Endorsements

Philologus, Julia, Nercus, and Olympas. Paul takes the time to record these names and many more as he writes the closing lines to his magnum opus, The Epistle to the Romans—and as he is inspired by the Holy Spirit. Dr. Weathers not only records names but also tells an inspiring and edifying story of those who worked behind the scenes as William Tyndale's accomplices. I often think of my debt to Tyndale as I read my English Bible. Now I know even more people to whom I owe a debt. This is not only a riveting tale from church history, it's an encouragement for us all to serve God with whatever gifts and capacity we have.

Dr. Stephen J. Nichols
President, Reformation Bible College
Chief Academic Officer, Ligonier Ministries

The Bible is full of unsung heroes, often mentioned only in the passing. Think of the unnamed women who ministered to the Lord Jesus Christ (see Luke 8:2–3). Eric Weathers has done the church a great service by digging behind the well-known history of Willian Tyndale, highlighting the men and women whose spiritual and material support enabled him to evade capture for ten years and give to the world, for the first time comprehensively, the word of God in the English language. These men and women were willing to risk their lives for the cause of the gospel. Without these unsung heroes, it is doubtful if Tyndale could have accomplished the work God entrusted to him. We rightly honour William Tyndale, but no less we should remember with the deepest gratitude those men and women who were, in God's providence, his godly accomplices.

Dr. Ian Hamilton
Professor of Historical and Pastoral Theology
Westminster Seminary, United Kingdom

Eric Weathers has identified many of the little-known individuals who made remarkable sacrifices to help the Bible become accessible in English. It is an encouraging account of God's unseen providence and God's unsung heroes who simply loved God, His Word, and His people—and in doing so, they changed the world. He reminds us that even today, those who love Christ and His Word can make a remarkable impact by serving in ways perhaps unseen by many—but treasured by the One who sees all things.

Dr. Mark Tatlock
President, The Master's Academy International

As a new widow, I found my hero through Eric's details of the secret and courageous ministry of the widow Margaret von Emerson. One woman, with six children and no husband, maintained a passion for Scripture that ignited her risk-taking willingness to steward her home and shelter Tyndale, the Bible-translating fugitive. Like Margaret, may every widow add joy to her grief, as she presses on to be a valuable link in Christ's works, trusting that He is worth more than any promise of earthly comfort or safety.

Brenda Hummert
Director of PrayerSHOP
Countryside Bible Church, Southlake, Texas

If you are one who "holds the rope while others go down the well," Eric Weathers's meticulously detailed history of William Tyndale's rope holders will encourage you. Not only will you read the rollicking tale of one of the most fascinating and important figures of the Protestant Reformation, but you will be reassured that your rope-holding truly matters.

Todd Friel
Executive Director of Fortis Institute
Host of Wretched TV and Radio
Pastor, Alpharetta Bible Church

William Tyndale's Accomplices is a powerful reminder that God uses ordinary people in extraordinary ways to advance His Word. This book is both historically rich and spiritually stirring, showing how courage, faith, and sacrifice changed the course of history. Readers will be inspired to see their own lives as vital links in God's global mission.

Dr. Dwight D. Ham, D.B.A., C.M.A.
Professor | Department of Business / Dept. Chair
The Master's University

Every tribe, tongue, people, and language. For those who respond to the Clarion call for the task remaining… an awareness and intimate knowledge of how the Bible was translated into our heart language adds fuel to the fire to see the same done for the over 3000 languages left to translate.

Dustin Elliott
Host, Unreached Podcast
Managing Director, Merrill Lynch

Dr. Weathers provides a detailed account of the trials and tribulations (and victories) that enabled William Tyndale to complete the translation of the New Testament from Greek to English. What a saga of twists and turns! But Weathers goes on to tell the story of the men and women who were behind Tyndale's effort. As a marketplace Christian, I was deeply encouraged by the writer's challenge to all believers to faithfully serve wherever God has placed us. We all have circles of influence where we "courageously serve Christ so that future generations will glorify the Lord." While the journey may bring "success, exhilaration, and courage, along with blessing and honor, it also [at times] comes with pain, sorrow, and grief." To God be the Glory!

Bob Doll
CEO, Crossmark Global Investments

William Tyndale's Accomplices is well-researched, compelling, and a must-read for anyone wanting to capture a full picture of the high personal costs many individuals paid in support of Tyndale's mission to give us the English translation of the Bible from the original languages. After reading this book, it will be impossible to take your English Bible for granted.

Adam Waller
Pastor, GraceLife London
Dean, of Hermeneia Bible Training Centre

As an Englishman, Tyndale is a hero and a legend of the faith for our country, but there are so many who stood with him and were vital in his mission to bring the scriptures into the language of the common person in England. Without his 'supporting cast,' Tyndale's work would never have been finished.

Ben Bradford
Pastor: Southam Road Evangelical Church
Oxfordshire, England

The motto of the 16th century Reformation was the Latin phrase *Post Tenebras Lux*—After Darkness, Light. Preceded by centuries of spiritual darkness, the light of God's Word dawned brightly on the English people thanks to the heroic translation work of William Tyndale. Before being captured in 1535 he spent the last 10 years of his young life on the run as a fugitive. As Eric Weathers's book reminds us—Tyndale did not, could not, have accomplished his mission without the help of others. Read and be introduced to these faithful saints who became Tyndale's supply chain. Today, those of us "called out of darkness into His marvelous light" owe them all a debt of thanks.

Wayne Knowles
Senior Development Officer
The Master's Academy International
Advisory Director - Sales
Confluence Investment Management

I very much enjoyed Weathers bringing his expertise in supply chain management to his research of *William Tyndale's Accomplices*. This book is much-needed encouragement, especially for those of us in the marketplace who seek to use our talent, time, and treasure to advance the Kingdom. Weathers's work highlights men and women throughout church history who used their secular skills, tenacity and wealth to support men like Tyndale to forever change the course of Christendom. *Soli Deo Gloria*!

Elizabeth G. Zellner
Esquire

William Tyndale's Accomplices serves as an encouragement and challenge to those in full-time secular roles as one considers that the Sovereign Lord uses all skill sets to further His Kingdom when one engages in opportunities for gospel advance. Weathers's careful highlights of the breadth of Tyndale's associates display the diversity of peoples used to accomplish a common goal.

Kerry S. Zellner, Jr.
Executive Engineer
Toyota Motor North America

Eric Weathers's excellent book mines the gold, outlining the contours of Tyndale's extraordinary life, drawing attention to his character and humility, and showing the rich significance of how, as he did what his hand found to do *with his might*, he found God raising up and providing co-labourers, comrades who ran with him and, as they fought alongside him, were together considerably more than the sum of their parts. Recommended.

Ben Virgo
Director, Christian Heritage London

Eric Weatherss's, *William Tyndale's Accomplices,* is a sober reminder through the documenting of William Tyndale's life, and his commitment to his Lord and His kingdom, of the reality and cost of the spiritual warfare for the eternal souls of men and the glory of God that is entailed in a commitment to Christ's Great Commission. But it is more than a well-written retelling of how God equipped and used a man immensely gifted by Him for his service. It is also a unique and extremely encouraging documentation of the many lesser-known believers, and some who are nameless faithful saints known only to God, who were called into a support role to help facilitate the ministry to which God had called William Tyndale. A calling every bit as important as the main calling of Tyndale himself. It is an encouraging reminder that there is no such thing as an insignificant Christian, that we all have a part to play in the building of God's kingdom in the world. May this book be an encouragement to believers to realize their lives can be used for an eternal purpose. And then to be a catalyst for them to fully commit their hearts and lives to the Lord, knowing He can and will use very ordinary believers in significant ways in sacrificial living, prayer, and giving to help facilitate the fulfilling of the Great Commission.

Dr. William Webster, PhD
Pastor of Grace Bible Church, Battleground, Washington
Author, *The Church of Rome at the Bar of History*

WILLIAM TYNDALE'S
ACCOMPLICES

Essential Partners of the
Forbidden English Bible Revealed

ERIC WEATHERS

THE
MASTER'S ACADEMY
INTERNATIONAL

tmai.org

William Tyndale's Accomplices:
Essential Partners of the Forbidden English Bible Revealed

Published by The Master's Academy International
13248 Roscoe Blvd
Sun Valley, CA 91352
tmai.org

Ancient English Scripture quotations are taken from *The 1526 Tyndale Bible New Testament*. Public Domain.

Modern Scripture quotations taken from the (LSB®) Legacy Standard Bible®, Copyright © 2021 by The Lockman Foundation. Used by permission. All rights reserved. Managed in partnership with Three Sixteen Publishing Inc., LSBible.org, and 316publishing.com.

ISBN: 978-1-967358-39-7

Published in the United States by The Master's Academy International

To Debbie, Erica, and David:
My faithful family and
fellow workers with the truth

Contents

Acknowledgements

I am thankful for my fellow workers in Christ for making *William Tyndale's Accomplices* possible. Special thanks to my wife, Debbie, for her love, encouragement, and the late nights spent editing the manuscript. Wayne Knowles, a businessman, church historian, and close brother in Christ, has been a constant source of motivation to strive for excellence. Chris Burnett's encouragement, "That book needs to be written, and you're going to write it!" Rick Kress ensured that key milestones and deadlines were met. Gurgen Sahakyan and Beaux Hargrove, master editors, have exceptional eyes for detail. Lastly, Wesley Mark transformed my imagination of the cover into a masterpiece.

E. W. unto the Reader

In the spirit of William Tyndale, who included a personal note to his readers in his 1534 translation of the New Testament titled, "W. T. Unto the Reader," I offer a message to you, the readers of this book.

On July 4, 2024, Debbie and I took a nine-hour flight to London to celebrate our fortieth wedding anniversary. We were excited to experience a self-guided walking tour focused on the Reformation, exploring the city where English Reformers served Christ five hundred years earlier. Pushing away from the gate in Dallas, Texas, I began reading a biography of Tyndale with his portrait on the cover as displayed in the National Portrait Gallery of London. Tyndale is painted sitting at a desk in a black outfit with a dark background. His face and hands are brightly painted, and his right index finger points directly to the Bible. With Tyndale's eyes fixed on the viewer, he invites all to pick it up and read.

After attending Sunday morning worship service at GraceLife London (the location of Hermeneia, a Bible school associated with The Master's Academy International), we walked ten minutes to Saint Bartholomew's Church in Smithfield. On the second floor of an apartment adjoining "St. Barts," Queen Mary stood watching martyrs being burned at the stake. Many other Reformers were burned in Smithfield long before Mary, including some discussed in this book.

Finally, we arrived at the National Portrait Gallery to see Tyndale's famous painting. However, our excitement turned to frustration as we searched every wall and could not locate the portrait of the man who risked his life to translate the Bible into English. An employee informed us that the portrait had been removed because they could not confirm that it was Tyndale, nor could they identify the painter. Granted, Tyndale did not allow images of himself while living in order to maintain his anonymity, but how could the Gallery remove a portrait so long accepted as depicting such an important figure in England's history?

As I reflected on Tyndale's portrait, I noticed the omission of a crucial detail—an element so integral to the English Reformation that drove me to write this book. As a former expert in global supply chain management, I wondered how an academic powerhouse fluent in eight languages, a preacher of the gospel, and the first man in history to translate the Bible from its original languages into English could also possess the skills to plan, fund, and communicate with people throughout Europe and England to smuggle 6,000 New Testaments into his home country, all while living as a fugitive?

Tyndale must have had help, but who were his supporters? I needed to uncover their identities and contributions. These godly saints would have been people willing to violate long-standing laws and to risk everything to produce and distribute Tyndale's English Bible. Absent from Tyndale's portrait are his supporters. Without the Lord providentially working through them, English readers in the sixteenth century and beyond would not have had access to God's Word in their own language. The cover of this book features a selection of Tyndale's mission-critical supply chain partners. To the left stand John and Anne Walsh, behind Tyndale is Humphrey Monmouth, followed by Margaret von Emerson next to Thomas Poyntz.

As you celebrate the 500th anniversary of William Tyndale's New Testaments arriving in England, and as you engage with this historical account of Tyndale and his associates, consider how God may be moving you to serve Him through your skills and expertise in the marketplace and public square. Not all Christians must go to a foreign nation to serve Him, but all Christians must fulfill the Great Commission by communicating the Word of God and using their gifts, skills, and expertise to make disciples of all nations. Perhaps your role in this mission is to pray for and support your brothers and sisters on the front lines in places you may never visit.

Could it be that you are called to enable others to translate the Bible and biblically sound theological works into foreign languages, and to facilitate the training of pastors/shepherds who will preach expository sermons from the authoritative Word of God? Could it be that your support could somehow help equip the saints to do the work of the ministry in local churches on a global scale? Thus, dear reader, I pray that you would courageously serve Christ so that future generations will glorify the Lord.

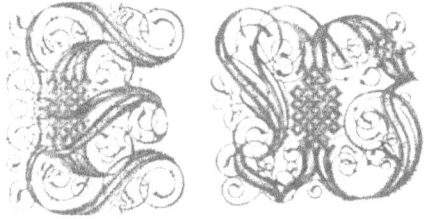

Introduction

In the years leading up to the sixteenth-century English Reformation, Roman Catholic governance exerted a pervasive influence over daily life. At the pinnacle of this feudal system were vast wealth-generating enterprises, including farmland where people labored to support their families. To provide for themselves, individuals swore allegiance to those who held power over their livelihoods. Opposition to Roman Catholic authorities was viewed as rebellion against God Himself. Consequently, the object of people's faith was not the God of the Bible, but rather a cold, lifeless system. They needed clear biblical doctrines and sound expository preaching because they were without genuine fellowship with God and His people. Their allegiance to their religion was seen as the only path to salvation, which was believed to be attainable only after enduring banishment in purgatory.

Biblical doctrines such as Christ's substitutionary atonement and justification by faith were as foreign to the people as the concept of landing a man on the moon. Their livelihoods were somewhat secure only to the extent that they upheld a false gospel, being burdened with unbiblical dogma. Very few had access to John Wycliffe's Bible, which he translated from Latin to English in the fourteenth century. Until that time in England's history, a biblical love for God and love for people was seen as hostility towards prevailing Roman Catholic obligations which were supported by the king and his loyal appointees. Any opposition to the Crown was considered heretical and seditious, often resulting in the death penalty.

English Bibles posed a threat to the culture because, as people engaged with Scripture, they began to perceive their religion and civilization as incompatible with God's Word. Archbishop Thomas Arundel warned that, as laypeople and the uneducated became familiar with the Bible, "they could support their private opinions by an appeal to the text of holy scripture."[1] Christians began to understand that the clear proclamation of the Bible was the sole authority to confront human depravity: "for not knowing about the righteousness of God and seeking to establish their own, they did not subject themselves to the righteousness of God" (Rom 10:3). Believers preached confession of Jesus as Lord leading to salvation (Rom 10:9), and they proclaimed justification by faith apart from works (Rom 4–5). This foreign preaching was viewed as a declaration of war. Roman Catholic leadership quickly retaliated.

In 1401, parliamentary law empowered Roman Catholic bishops to imprison and burn English Bible translators as well as those who read their Bibles. In November 1407, Archbishop Arundel convened his leadership team in Oxford, England, to formulate ordinances to thwart the proliferation of English Bibles and tracts. By 1408, the council approved thirteen laws known as the Constitutions of Oxford. These decrees prohibited the translation, printing, distribution, and preaching of the Bible in Latin or the vernacular language without official approval. Only those recognized as parish priests or licensed individuals were permitted to lead church services, and even they were forbidden from explaining the Bible outside of the ancient traditions passed down through generations. Violators of the Constitutions faced severe penalties, including excommunication and punishments deemed fitting for heresy,[2] which could lead to death by burning at the stake.

Undaunted, those in William Tyndale's support network were moved by the authority of God's Word; they pledged their allegiance to Jesus Christ, the King of kings and Lord of lords. This unwavering devotion compelled them to explore the Bible—even at the risk of losing everything, including their own lives. However, while enriching,

1   Margaret Deanesly, *The Lollard Bible and Other Medieval Biblical Versions* (Cambridge: Cambridge University Press, 1920), 295.

2   Deanesly, *Lollard Bible*, 296.

the early translation made by John Wycliffe, referred to as the "Lollard Bible," was archaic, hard to find, and difficult for most English people to read. Believers earnestly prayed for a Bible in their common language, one that even a minimally educated farm boy could easily comprehend (Col 1:9–14). They sought to be trained in righteousness so that future generations could be equipped for every good work (2 Tim 3:16–17).

God providentially appointed William Tyndale to translate the New Testament from Greek into English, even though his translation made him a criminal. The Lord also assigned courageous individuals to print, smuggle, and distribute these Bibles throughout the English-speaking world. In 1524 and the years following, he was blessed with astute believers with the financial resources necessary to underwrite the costs of translation as well as the associated expenses within the supply chain from printing to smuggling and distributing Bibles. This made them accomplices to Tyndale's crime, but their daring efforts ensured that common people across England, Wales, and Scotland would know more of the Bible than their religious leaders, including the pope.

William Tyndale's Accomplices encourages readers to live courageously for the gospel of Christ, no matter the consequences. As Tyndale and his associates navigate typical human experiences—joy, setbacks, success, persecution, and the shared emotions of rejoicing and mourning—readers will encounter passages from Tyndale's Bible translation that may have offered them encouragement during those times. As you read, you might reflect on portions of God's Word that would have uplifted you in similar circumstances.

The book has two primary objectives. First, it informs readers by recounting the historical challenges faced by Tyndale and the individuals who risked everything to produce and distribute the English Bible. Second, it aims to inspire believers to fearlessly trust in God's providence by exploring practical strategies that equip shepherd-expositors with the tools needed to faithfully preach God's Word in local churches worldwide.

As you serve faithfully in your home church, loving God, His Word, and His people, be ready to risk everything to ensure that future generations are equipped to pursue the Great Commission until the end of the age.

If you are in Christ, you are His fellow worker. The question is: how can God advance the Great Commission through you by your connections with others within your circles of influence—your coworkers, friends, and neighbors who urgently need to hear the gospel and receive God's gracious pardon for their sins?

In the following chapters, you will meet Tyndale's co-laborers in Christ: widows, cloth workers, law students, brickmakers, lawyers, pastors, ironmongers, theologians, dock workers, printers, governors, business administrators, knights, aldermen, mayors, logistics experts, university students, evangelists, and men and women of significant wealth, including those whose titles resemble modern Chief Executive Officers. You will also encounter people with extreme wealth who modeled 1 Timothy 6:17–19. You will discover prison executives, sheriffs, merchants, salespeople, smugglers, and individuals closely associated with the king and his closest advisors.

Driven by love for God and people (Matt 22:37–40), these men and women risked everything for the English Bible. Some lost their families, others lost their livelihoods and lives; some jeopardized their multinational business enterprises, while others put their print shops on the line. Those faithful generations are gone, and now it is your turn. Fear not, for Jesus is with you until your last breath, even to the end of the age (Matt 28:20).

Most chapters start with William Tyndale's translation of the New Testament. Take your time to read the text as if it were your first encounter in 1526. Please appreciate the accessibility of the language and the clarity of the message. When reading Tyndale's translation with children, encourage them to sound out each word. Help them grasp the meaning and its relevance to their lives, even if you need to reference a modern translation.

CHAPTER 1

Patterns of God's Providence

*I cōmende unto you Phebe oure suster (which is a minister of
the cōgregacion of Chencrea) that ye receave her in the lorde as it
becōmeth saynctes, and that ye assist her, in whatsoever busines
she neadeth of youre ayde. For she hath suckered many, and myne
awne silfe also. Grete Prisca and Aquila my helpers in Christ Iesu:
which have for my lyfe layde doune their awne neckes. unto whom
not I only geve thankes: but also the congregaciōs of the gentils.
Lyke wyse grete all the company that is ī their housse.*
Romans 16:1–5[1]

Marvel not at the brilliance of William Tyndale, the scholar who
translated the Bible into the common language of the people amid
the political and religious upheaval of sixteenth-century England. His
work illuminated the path of salvation, delivering from despair and offering joy for young and old alike. His craftsmanship, sharp words, and newly
coined phrases were a stroke of genius, bringing the Word of God into
sharper focus for the ordinary person. Rather than marveling at the man,
rejoice in God's providence in using his gifts and the company he kept.

As mentioned earlier, Tyndale was not the first to translate the Bible
into English; he followed John Wycliffe, who translated the Latin Bible
into English in the 1300s. However, while the embers of Wycliffe's
work still flickered and called for converts, Tyndale produced the first
translation directly from the original Greek and some Hebrew texts.

---

[1]   When Tyndale published his translation of the New Testament, English spelling differed from
modern spelling conventions in notable ways. Tyndale's spelling, a product of its time, is archaic and
inconsistent; since the letter *J* had not yet been widely adopted, the text represents *J* with an *I* in both
upper- and lowercase.

As Wycliffe's Bible began to be preached in England, the realities of life—political, societal, and religious—were opened to scrutiny, even by those considered the lowest of society who encountered these truths for the first time. Wycliffe, his followers, and their works were labeled "Lollards," a derogatory term used by Catholic adherents to mock what they perceived as the unorthodox and simplistic beliefs of those who did not conform to their way of life.

Wycliffe's work was handwritten, which hindered its distribution and rendered it illegible to some. Additionally, rapid developments in the English language made many of Wycliffe's terms archaic. As will be seen, the most direct attack on Wycliffe's work came from an edict issued at Oxford University, where he had once served as a theology professor.

The ruling class in England found the "Lollard Bible" unacceptable, particularly because it aimed to enlighten even the "lowest" members of society, freeing them from the grip of Roman Catholic control. Questions arose as traditions and practices prescribed by the papacy and its prelates were not supported by Wycliffe's translation. This Bible challenged the pope and the hierarchical authority of the Catholic governance over the nation by its sheer silence on certain practices. Sermons proclaiming that true power comes from God, not worldly institutions or individuals, were met with fatal threats and sanctions designed to keep God's Word from the common English people.

Parliamentary law in 1401 permitted Roman Catholic bishops to arrest and burn English Bible translators and anyone who read their works. One such priest, William Sawtrey, inspired by John Wycliffe's fourteenth-century translation of the Latin Bible into English, confronted the Archbishop of Canterbury, Thomas Arundell, regarding the authority of Scripture. Sawtrey pronounced God's judgment not only on Arundell, but also on the clergy and the king. Shortly thereafter, Sawtrey inhaled the flames of death at Smithfield.[2] Seven years

---

2   Brian Moynahan, *God's Bestseller* (New York: St. Martin's Press, 2003), xxii.

later, Arundell enacted the Constitutions of Oxford, which mandated, "that no man, hereafter, by his own authority translate any text of the Scripture into English or any other tongue…." Repeat offenders were to be burned.[3]

For the next 118 years, religious leaders and secular officials conspired to prevent the common English people from accessing God's Word. Bolstered by the pope, the king, and the laws of the realm, they made every effort to stop people from reading Scripture—the power of God for salvation to everyone who believes (Rom 1:16).

A Pauline Precedent for Tyndale

As Tyndale immersed himself in the Scriptures—studying each book, chapter, line, and word, he himself was swayed and shaped by God. In effect, the one who produced an English translation was transformed by God from a scholar of great intellect to a humble believer, determined to guard the treasure of sacred truth, seeking to influence others to do their part as well.

Such words, thoughts, and actions of a man so faithful and effective in the study, translation, and transmission of the very words of God must have had a precedent.

The Apostle Paul experienced similar miserable conditions in Acts 18:1 as he departed from Athens and traveled to Corinth, arguably the most depraved city of the first century, where he penned the book of Romans in approximately AD 57. From 1 Corinthians 2:3, we learn that Paul entered Corinth feeling weak, fearful, and trembling. Yet, by God's wisdom, he arrived in the city which resembled the kinds of sins he described in Romans 1:18–32. He knew what it was like to minister among a culture beset by moral bankruptcy, where people could not distinguish between right and wrong. Paul's solution to their depravity

---

3   Moynahan, *God's Bestseller*, xxii.

was to proclaim the very words of God through a faithful messenger, supported by a network of dependable risk-takers committed to the Great Commission.

The first four and a half verses of Romans 16 describe two practical ways to be a reliable servant of Christ in difficult circumstances. Paul begins by commending Phoebe, a faithful sister in Christ and a member of the church in Cenchrea, located about eight miles from Corinth and approximately seven hundred miles from Rome. He urged the house churches in Rome to welcome her warmly. Although Paul had never visited these churches in person since his travels were hindered by the Holy Spirit (Acts 18:21; Rom 1:10; 15:22–24, 30–32), nevertheless, in Romans 1:7, Paul states that he persistently prayed for "all who are beloved of God in Rome, called as saints." In the next verse, he thanks God because their "faith is being proclaimed throughout the whole world." Although most Roman believers had never met Paul, the Lord grew the church to the extent that their love for Him and for people had a worldwide impact for the sake of the gospel (Rom 1:8).

Similar to William Tyndale, who could not preach and disciple in England, Paul was unable to directly disciple the people in Rome (Rom 1:10–13). Therefore, under the authority of the Holy Spirit, he wrote this epistle to proclaim the righteousness of God and how He saves people from His eternal wrath. The Book of Romans is arguably the most important letter in human history; 1,500 years later, it became the primary document that exposed the centuries-long apostasy of Roman Catholicism.

In AD 57, after completing his letter, Paul faced a dilemma: who could he trust to deliver it to Rome, ensuring the necessary financial means? Should it be a private militia or a team of experienced men familiar with the seven hundred-mile journey from Corinth to Rome? While Paul does not explicitly state it, his language suggests that Phoebe was the courier. Consequently, historians and commentators agree that she probably delivered the letter to the original recipients: the house churches in Rome.[4] If Paul entrusted Phoebe with his letter, she would have to undertake a perilous journey by land and sea, with the added dangers of being a woman. However, Paul's recommendation meant that Christians along the way could trust her in their homes.

What if she became fearful and abandoned her mission? What if she changed her mind midway through the journey? What if she was distracted by dangers or temptations? If that happened, God provided her with a way of escape (1 Cor 10:13). She needed to be strong and courageous, laying aside all the encumbrances of sin, fixing her eyes on Jesus (Heb 12:1–2). Phoebe had to trust in the Lord wholeheartedly, not relying on her own understanding, knowing that acknowledging Him would make her paths straight (Prov 3:5–6). She presented her body as a living sacrifice, holy and pleasing to God in her spiritual service of worship (Rom 12:1–2). The letter she carried assured her that nothing could separate her from God's love—not even peril or sword (Rom 8:31–39).

Paul commends "our sister Phoebe" to the Roman churches. "Commend" can also be rendered as "recommend," literally meaning to "stand with."[5] Because Paul stands with and trusts Phoebe, the Romans are encouraged to receive her with open arms as their trustworthy sister in Christ. "Sister" expresses endearment, indicating she is part of their church family. In verse 1, Paul establishes Phoebe's reputation, describing her as "a servant of the church," specifically the church in Cenchrea, located eight miles from Corinth. Before Phoebe could be trusted in a foreign culture, she first had to demonstrate faithfulness in her home church. Just before reading the first fifteen

---

4   Douglas J. Moo, *The Epistle to the Romans*, The New International Commentary on the New Testament (Grand Rapids: Eerdmans, 1996), 913; John MacArthur Jr., *Romans 9–16*, The MacArthur New Testament Commentary (Chicago: Moody, 1994), 359; Leon Morris, *The Epistle to the Romans*, The Pillar New Testament Commentary (Grand Rapids: Eerdmans, 1988), 528.

5   "συνίστημι," ed. Spiros Zodhiates, *The Complete Word Study Dictionary: New Testament* (Iowa Falls, IA: World Bible Publishers, 1992), 1344.

chapters aloud, the church witnessed Phoebe delivering the letter from Paul's hand to their reader.

They listened to the entire book before Paul highlighted Phoebe's significance to him and to them. Paul's recommendation of Phoebe includes two key expectations for the Roman believers. First, he instructs them to "receive her in the Lord," meaning they should accept her as they would accept Jesus Himself. Additionally, they were to receive Phoebe "in a manner worthy of the saints." This should evoke thoughts of Matthew 25 and the final judgment at the end of the age. According to Matthew 25:34–40, welcoming Phoebe in a manner worthy of the saints equates to receiving Jesus Himself. Paul's request aligns perfectly with that of Jesus: to serve those who serve God. As will be shown, many of Tyndale's faithful associates exemplified Jesus' message in Matthew 25:40.

Paul urges them to "help Phoebe." The Greek word *paristēmi* means to "stand next to," "be present," or "stand by someone;" it means to "put at someone's disposal to assist them in whatever they need."[6] To what extent should they help Phoebe? They were to help her "in whatever matter she may have need" (Rom 16:2), treating her as if she were Jesus Himself. In verse 2, Paul provides two reasons for helping Phoebe. First, she has been a "helper" (meaning "benefactor" or "patroness") to many. She was entrusted with carrying Paul's Letter to the Romans because he knew she had faithfully supported many saints back home in Cenchrea. The second reason is that she had also been a helper and patroness to Paul himself. Though she was a stranger to the churches in Rome, she was their sister in Christ and a servant of her home church; she was a woman of means and a benefactress to Paul and many others.

---

6   "παρίστημι," Walter Bauer, Frederick W. Danker, William Arndt, and F. Wilbur Gingrich, *A Greek-English Lexicon of the New Testament and Other Early Christian Literature*, 3rd ed. (Chicago: University of Chicago Press, 2000), 778.

Provision of Aquila and Priscilla

In Acts 18:2, Claudius expelled all Jews from Italy, including Aquila and his wife, Priscilla. This event providentially brought them to Corinth, where they joined the Apostle Paul in advancing the gospel as fellow workers. All three shared the trade of leatherworking, referred to as "tentmakers" in Tyndale's English text. Aquila and Priscilla were successful business owners who worked diligently for the Lord. They hired Paul, an expert tentmaker, to assist them and provided him with a safe place to call home. In return, Paul contributed to the prosperity of their business while they cared for his needs. He discipled them, preparing them for a lifetime of ministry, which allowed them to host house churches in Corinth, Ephesus, and Rome. They also encouraged a man named Apollos by explaining to him "the way of God more accurately" (Acts 18:26).

Later, in Romans 16:3–5, Paul extended greetings to Priscilla and Aquila, referring to them as his "fellow workers in Christ Jesus." He often recognized both men and women for working alongside him to advance the gospel. "Fellow workers in Christ" indicates his respect for their service, which he regarded as equal to his own. Their ministry was distinct from Paul's, meaning that Priscilla and Aquila served the Lord in their unique ways. As his fellow workers, their labor was mission-critical. Priscilla and Aquila are known for a second significant detail: Paul states, "For my life they risked their own necks" (Rom 16:4). Just as Paul expressed gratitude for this couple, so did "all the churches of the Gentiles" for their willingness to protect Paul from a premature and violent death. While we cannot pinpoint the exact instances they saved his life, much of what we know about Priscilla and Aquila comes from Acts 18–19, where their reliability is evident.

Business professionals like Priscilla and Aquila played a critical role in the foundation of the church in the first century. God used them as His means by which churches further equipped the saints for the work of the ministry (Eph 4:12–16). That same model continued throughout church history; in the early sixteenth century, God provided William Tyndale with believers who generated wealth in the marketplace to ensure the careful production and distribution of Bibles.

God compelled and equipped William Tyndale to present His Word in plain English, declaring that His governance extends over all creation, including the actions of both good and evil men. He aimed to remove barriers of ignorance and language in England. The Sovereign King over all nations worked—and still works—to save and restore His people through a plan in which no detail is insignificant.[7] Even seemingly mundane aspects of Tyndale's life exemplify God's creative providence, fitting him for service and placing him alongside other faithful workers to fulfill His plan.

God's Provision for William Tyndale's Early Years

Following the milestones of a man who undertook anonymity for the sake of his mission can challenge the best of historians. The desire for anonymity seemed to be a common family practice. William's grandfather settled in Dursley to avoid conflict and adopted a new last name—a pseudonym that William later used to safeguard his own identity.

According to John Foxe, historian and contemporary of Tyndale, he "was born about the borders of Wales"[8] in Gloucestershire near the River Severn around 1494. J. F. Mozley argues that Tyndale's Oxford master's degree, awarded on July 2, 1515, legally prohibited graduation before the age of twenty. Thus, he must have been born no later than 1495, with 1494 being the likely year of his birth.[9] David Daniell affirms Mozley's 1494 estimated year and admits that there

---

7   For an understanding of the doctrine of divine governance, see John MacArthur and Richard Mayhue, eds., *Biblical Doctrine: A Systematic Summary of Bible Truth* (Wheaton, IL: Crossway, 2017), 221.

8   John Foxe, *The Acts and Monuments of John Foxe*, 8 vols. (London: R. B. Seeley and W. Burnside, 1837–39), 5:114.

9   J. F. Mozley, *William Tyndale* (New York: The Macmillan Company, 1937), 1.

are no records identifying the precise place of his birth, notwithstanding Foxe's assertion.[10]

A footnote in John Foxe's *Acts and Monuments* states that William Tyndale was a descendant of Robert Baron de Tyndale of Longly Castle in Northumberland. This ancestor moved approximately three hundred miles south to Gloucestershire to avert the wars of York and Lancaster, and he adopted the name "Hutchins" to avoid aggravating tensions between rival families. Robert, William Tyndale's grandfather, married Alicia Hunt, the sole heiress of her father, known as Hunt from Nibley (near Dursley).[11] Further, Tyndale's Oxford studies suggest that he likely came from a financially stable family that could support his costs of living and education while in school.

As shown in *The Military Survey of Gloucestershire*, which details residents' assets and land holdings in 1522, the Tyndale family had properties in Hurst, Stinchcombe, and Breadstone.[12] This evidence suggests that Tyndale was born in the Gloucestershire region, close to his grandparents' residence in Dursley, about one mile from Nibley Knoll, the site of the 111-foot Tyndale Monument, a few miles east of Wales and within the Cotswolds.[13] The Gloucestershire area, renowned for its fertile soils in the Severn Vale, lies adjacent to the River Severn, which links its ports to trade routes throughout the region and beyond. Key industries included the cultivation of various food crops and sheep farms famous for their wool production, which significantly contributed to the local economy and was essential to Tyndale's supply chain. Additionally, the region was known for its timber and iron ore resources, which provided profitable opportunities for business owners,

---

10   David Daniell, *William Tyndale: A Biography* (New Haven, CT: Yale University Press, 2001), 9.

11   Daniell, *William Tyndale*, 9; John Foxe, *Acts and Monuments* 5:114–15n3.

12   R. W. Hoyle, ed., *The Military Survey of Gloucestershire, 1522* (Bristol: Bristol and Gloucestershire Archaeological Society, 1993), 138, 146.

13   Daniell, *William Tyndale*, 9.

supported the manufacturing of farm implements, and ensured a steady income for blacksmiths and laborers.

David Daniell confirms that the Tyndale family held considerable real estate and were wealthy merchants who carried sway over the local economy and were amiable to the teachings of the Reformation. His brother Thomas was the landowner, while another brother of his, Edward, was an expert in trade.[14] Perhaps God later used Thomas to finance William's efforts and Edward to collaborate with others to smuggle Bibles into England.

Conclusive information about William Tyndale's activities from 1515 to 1522 is not definitive. Historian Dr. Brian Buxton reports that Tyndale was ordained as a priest in London in 1515, but he admits that records of that appointment are missing. It is possible that this was a different man also named William Tyndale who died in 1523.[15]

Pondering God's Providence

As the precedence of the Apostle Paul attests, God communicated His plan to Paul, and then Paul dispatched a faithful messenger. Additionally, his associates worked to support the effort. As we turn the page to the story of William Tyndale, we find that the same holds true in the sixteenth century. That same message and divine directive drove the messenger, William Tyndale, to overrule Roman Catholicism, the pope, the king, and his loyalists so that the Word of God would be studied and preached for centuries in England and around the world. Tyndale did not take on this initiative alone. Just like Paul, he also depended on a team of faithful believers who labored with him in this work, as we will see in the following chapters. So far, we have examined only his beginning.

---

14 Daniell, *William Tyndale*, 10–11.

15 Brian Buxton, *At the House of Thomas Poyntz: The Betrayal of William Tyndale with the Consequences for an English Merchant and His Family* (Lavenham, UK: Brian Buxton, 2013), 23.

Relishing God's Providence Today

Those who are in Christ are His fellow workers. God continues to use Christians to advance the Great Commission by bringing unbelievers into their homes to participate in enriching conversations around the dinner table. These could be coworkers, friends, and neighbors who need to hear the gospel and become fellow workers in Christ.

CHAPTER 2

Foundations of Tyndale's Trusted Network

For by grace are ye made safe throwe fayth, and that not of youre selves: For it is the gyfte of God, and commeth not of workes, lest eny man shulde bost hym silfe. For we are his worckmanshippe, created in Christ Iesu unto good workes, unto the which god ordeyned us before, that we shulde walke in them.
Ephesians 2:8–10

After graduating from Oxford University and spending time at the University of Cambridge, Tyndale returned to the pasturelands of Gloucestershire, England, where fertile ground and access to trade routes facilitated the exchange of wool and other essential goods. Little Sodbury, approximately 13 miles from his birthplace, proved to be the seedbed and trailhead of William Tyndale's mission.

John Foxe notes that after "being further ripened in the knowledge of God's Word," Tyndale began working for Sir John and Lady Anne Walsh in 1522.[1] Tutoring the Walsh children at Little Sodbury Manor,[2] the home of John and Anne, provided the fertile ground for the scholar to grow in his convictions and to connect with people of influence.

---

1   Daniell, *William Tyndale*, 55; Mozley, *William Tyndale*, 23.

2   Little Sodbury Manor is a three-story home that was renovated in the 1920s, but much of its original 17,385-square-foot structure remains intact. See Jennifer Tzeses, *King Henry VIII and Anne Boleyn Lived in This $10.5 Million Castle*, accessed August 20, 2025, https://www.architecturaldigest.com/story/king-henry-viii-anne-boleyn-castle.

Brian Buxton notes that many university graduates relied on patrons for support.[3] Scholars without university appointments often sought assistance from affluent patrons, similar to the aid given to Desiderius Erasmus by Lord Mountjoy, who was present at King Henry VIII's coronation in 1509 and knighted the following day.[4] Understanding how the Lord may have connected the Tyndale and Walsh families opens the door to seeing how He used them to help lay the foundation for William Tyndale's translation of the Bible during his time working for them.

There is a direct link between the kind Walsh hospitality in 1522 and millions of people around the world who have now called on the name of Christ for more than 500 years since Tyndale's Bibles were smuggled into England (Rom 10:11–17).

Anne Poyntz-Walsh

Understanding that Sir John Walsh had two wives, both named Anne, is necessary to accurately follow the relationships and means God provided for Tyndale's work.

Walsh's first wife, Anne Poyntz-Walsh, was the daughter of Sir Robert Poyntz of Iron Acton in Gloucestershire, England, about six miles east of Little Sodbury.[5] John Walsh Sr. inherited Little Sodbury Manor through his marriage to the heiress of the property, which was then

---

3   Buxton, *At the House of Thomas Poyntz*, 24.

4   Heather Y. Wheeler, "King Henry VIII Coronation 24th June 1509," Tudor Nation, last updated July 12, 2024, https://www.tudornation.com/king-henry-viii-coronation/.

5   As will be shown, God used the Poyntz family to play a significant role in William Tyndale's life. They were close to King Henry VIII; further, Thomas Poyntz lived in the English House in Antwerp which was William Tyndale's secret residence when he was arrested on August 23, 1535. Robert Poyntz' mother was Margaret Woodville (Poyntz), the illegitimate daughter of Anthony Wydville (alternatively, Woodville), Second Earl of Rivers. Anthony was the brother of Queen Elizabeth (Woodville) who was the wife of King Edward IV. Margaret was Anthony Wydville's only child and was married to Sir Robert Poyntz, Sheriff of Southampton, who was present at King Edward's funeral in 1483.

handed down to his son, Sir John Walsh, a Knight of Gloucestershire who served as King Henry VIII's Champion at his coronation in 1509.[6] John Abernathy Kingdon writes: "As a family it is clear that the Poyntzes of Iron Acton were well regarded by the Sovereigns Henry VII and VIII."[7] As William Tyndale's network solidified, these family relationships proved providential for the translation of the English Bible and for the rest of his life. John's first wife, Anne, bore him a single child, Margaret, before passing away at an early age.[8]

Lady Anne Dinley-Walsh

Sir John's second marriage was to Lady Anne Dinley-Walsh, the daughter of John Dinley of Hampshire. This is the Lady Anne Walsh who, with Sir John, hired William Tyndale to tutor their children in 1522.

Sir John Walsh

Prior to William's employment at his manor, Sir John was associated with the Tyndale family as well as King Henry VIII. The "stalwart and expert man-at-arms" was recognized "as having been champion to Henry VIII," whom the king knighted.[9]

---

6   Robert Demaus, *William Tyndale: A Biography* (London: The Religious Tract Society, [1871]), 41; Foxe, *Acts and Monuments*, 5:115; John Maclean, ed., "Transactions of the Bristol and Gloucestershire Archaeological Society in 1888–9, Proceedings at the Spring Meeting at Chipping Sodbury, On Tuesday, May 29th, 1888," *Transactions of the Bristol and Gloucestershire Archaeological Society* 13 (1888–89): 3–4.

7   John Abernathy Kingdon, *Incidents in the Lives of Thomas Poyntz and Richard Grafton* (London: Privately Printed by Rixon & Arnold, 1895), 3.

8   Andrew Hope. Personal email dated September 8, 2024. "It is now clear that Sir John Walsh's first wife, Anne Poyntz, died some years before Tyndale arrived at Little Sodbury. The Lady Anne Walsh present when Tyndale arrived was Sir John Walsh's second wife, Anne Dinle, or Dinley, or Dingley (etc.), Virtually all Tyndale biographies are wrong in this respect. The relevant information was available in print in the 19th century, but was missed. I am in debt to Brian Buxton for bringing it to my attention. It is important because the Dingleys were much more religiously conservative than the Poyntz family. I always thought it was inconceivable that Anne Poyntz could have expressed the views attributed to Lady Anne Walsh by Foxe." Cf. Maclean, "Transactions at Chipping Sodbury," 4.

9   Demaus, *William Tyndale*, 41.

According to *The Military Survey of Gloucestershire, 1522*, John Walsh held the title of "Crown Steward for the Berkeley estate (a position he had handed over in 1519 to Edward Tyndale, William's brother) and auditor and steward of Tewkesbury Abbey (which post, again, he handed over to Edward Tyndale in 1536 at the Dissolution), he was twice High Sheriff of Gloucestershire."[10] For the sake of emphasis, it is important to note that three years before William Tyndale began working for Sir John, Walsh surrendered his Berkeley Estate responsibilities to Edward Tyndale, who then assumed responsibilities for the Tewkesbury Abbey the same year as his brother's martyrdom in 1536.

Controversies at the Dinner Table

The Walsh friendships with prominent members of high society provided Tyndale with a seat at a table surrounded by "abbots, deans, archdeacons, with divers other doctors, and great beneficed men; who there, together with Master Tyndale sitting at the same table, did use many times to enter communication, and talk of learned men, as of Luther and of Erasmus; also of divers other controversies and questions upon the Scripture."[11]

Interestingly, the well-connected Walshes hosted an overnight visit with their friend, King Henry VIII, and his wife, Anne Boleyn, on August 23, 1535, though it was years after Tyndale's residence there—about three months after William Tyndale was arrested in Antwerp.[12] Two days later, Thomas Poyntz, in whose home Tyndale resided at the time of his arrest, had sent an urgent letter, dated August 25, to his brother John Poyntz, hoping to leverage his network's influence with

---

10   Daniell, *William Tyndale*, 54.

11   Foxe, *Acts and Monuments*, 5:115.

12   Demaus, *William Tyndale*, 425.

the king to secure Tyndale's release from imprisonment from Castle Vilvoorde.[13]

At the dinner table, heated discussions frequently escalated into debates about the "new learning" from scholars like Martin Luther and Erasmus.[14] Tyndale supported his arguments by appealing to the authority of Scripture. Over time, these interactions unsettled many guests and even placed the Walshes' lives at risk.

In 1530, eight years later, Tyndale reflects on his conversations at the Walshes' table with Roman Catholic prelates and their lack of sound biblical exegesis. He recalled that universities forbade a man from studying Scripture "until he be noselled in heathen learning eight or nine years, and armed with false principles; with which he is clean shut out of the understanding of the scripture."[15] Tyndale testified that "when a man first enters the university he shall not defame the university, whatsoever he seeth. And when he taketh first degree, he is sworn that he shall hold none opinion condemned by the church; but what such opinions be, that he shall not know."[16] Tyndale further noted that when a man is admitted to the study of divinity, Scripture itself

is locked up with such false expositions, and with false principles of natural philosophy, that they cannot enter in, they go about the outside, and dispute all their lives about words and vain opinions, pertaining as much unto the healing of a man's heel, as health of his soul: provided yet alway, lest God give his singular grace unto any

13   Kingdon, *Incidents in the Lives*, front matter.

14   Marcus Loane, *Masters of the English Reformation* (1954; repr., Edinburgh: Banner of Truth Trust, 2005), 64.

15   William Tyndale, *The Practice of Prelates*, in *The Works of William Tyndale*, vol. 2, *Expositions and Notes on Sundry Portions of the Holy Scriptures, Together with the Practice of Prelates*, ed. Henry Walter (1849; repr., Edinburgh: Banner of Truth Trust, 2010), 291.

16   Ibid.

person, that none may preach except he be admitted of
the bishops.[17]

The Bearing of Secret Grudges

That these religious priests and bishops were "noselled" from God's
Word indicates that Tyndale's exposition of Scripture sounded foreign to
them. To these academically advanced yet scripturally ill-informed men,
it made a sort of twisted sense to view Tyndale as a heretic. John Foxe
noted that Tyndale "spared not to show unto them simply and plainly
his judgment in matters, as he thought; and when they at any time did
vary from Tyndale in opinions and judgment, he would show them in
the book, and lay plainly before them the open and manifest places of
the Scriptures, to confute their errors, and confirm his sayings."[18] As
the Walshes entertained their guests at Little Sodbury Manor, they had
a front row seat to this kind of sound biblical exposition and preaching from Tyndale. No doubt, their senses caught the disapproving
looks and murmurs signaling strife between Tyndale and their guests.
Nevertheless, as Foxe notes, all those present at the table with Tyndale
"continued ... for a certain season, reasoning and contending together
divers and sundry times, till at length they waxed weary, and bare a secret
grudge in their hearts against him."[19] Because the Walshes' dinner guests
offered "crafty persuasions" and unsound opposing comments, Tyndale
was convinced to find a way to provide a Bible for his detractors so
that they could read and understand the truth. Perhaps his thoughts
about their lost souls were guided by the Greek to English translation
on Hebrews 4:12 he would go on to complete: "For the word of God is
living and active and sharper than any two-edged sword, and piercing as

---

17   Tyndale, *The Practice of Prelates, in Expositions and Notes*, 291.
18   Foxe, *Acts and Monuments*, 5:115.
19   Ibid.

far as the division of soul and spirit, of both joints and marrow, and able to judge the thoughts and intentions of the heart."

By such conversations, God emboldened William Tyndale at the Walsh home. He understood that the Father had given Jesus all authority in heaven and earth to make disciples (Matt 28:18–20), and that no priest, bishop, or so-called "pope" could diminish His Lordship over the affairs of men.

An Outburst of Blasphemy and Growing Resistance

Tyndale's fearlessness is evident in his complete confidence in God's Word during his disputes with one well-educated man. Foxe records:

> [Tyndale] drave him to that issue [the authority of Scripture], that the said great doctor burst out into these blasphemous words, and said, "We were better to be without God's laws than the popes." Master Tyndale, hearing this, full of godly zeal, and not bearing that blasphemous saying, replied again, and said, "I defy the pope, and all his laws;" and further added, that if God spared him life, ere many years he would cause a boy that driveth the plough, to know more of the Scripture than he did.[20]

Shortly before Tyndale made his bold proclamation, Erasmus expressed similar thoughts in his 1516 work, *Novum Instrumentum omne*, writing, "I would to God ye ploughman would sing a text of scripture at his plowbeme and that the Weaver at his loowme with this would drive away the tediousness of tyme."[21]

---

20   Foxe, *Acts and Monuments*, 5:117.

21   Charles C. Butterworth and Allan G. Chester, *George Joye: 1495?–1553: A Chapter in the History of the English Bible and the English Reformation* (Philadelphia: University of Pennsylvania Press, 1962), 28.

Increasingly, though, Tyndale experienced resistance; such was the case even from the Walshes on one occasion after meeting with learned men at a banquet, where great doctors talked "at will and pleasure, uttering their blindness and ignorance without any resistance or gainsaying."[22]

After the occasion, Lady Walsh questioned William and his teachings, living up to Tyndale's impression of her as a "wise," and "stout" woman. The Walshes recounted their meeting with the great doctors to William. Tyndale, in typical fashion, addressed their concerns with Scripture. Like the qualified elder described in Titus 1:9, he held firmly to the truth of God's Word, exhorting in sound doctrine and reproving those who contradicted it. Moreover, Lady Walsh countered, "There was such a doctor who may dispend a hundred pounds, and another two hundred pounds, and another three hundred pounds: and what! were it reason, think you, that we should believe you before them?" Praise the Lord for Lady Walsh! God used her to further sanctify William from temptation toward pride or self-importance. Tyndale wisely refrained from responding to her until the right moment, for, as Foxe revealed, William's mindset at the time was that "he saw it would not avail."[23]

Later, after Tyndale completed his Latin to English translation of Erasmus's *Enchiridion Militis Christiani* ("Handbook of a Christian Knight") in 1504,[24] he gave a copy to John and Anne, but "after they had read and well perused the same, the doctorly prelates were no more so often called to the house, neither had they the cheer and countenance when they came, as before they had ... at last utterly withdrew, and came no more there."[25] The priests and doctorly prelates no longer had sway with Sir John and Lady Anne.

---

22 Foxe, *Acts and Monuments*, 5:115.

23 Ibid., 5:116.

24 Desiderius Erasmus, *Enchiridion Militis Christiani*, trans. anonymous (London: Methuen & Co., 1905).

25 Foxe, *Acts and Monuments*, 5:116.

Reports of Heresy

Feeling unwelcome, Tyndale's adversaries decided to unite against him. As their animosity grew, they gathered in "alehouses and other places … affirming that his sayings were heresy …, and so accused him secretly to the chancellor, and others of the bishop's officers."[26] Tyndale, who had probably already translated Jesus' warning in John 16:3–4, would not have been surprised by their hatred: "And suche thinges will they do unto you because they have not knowen the father nether yet me. But these thynges have I tolde you that when the houre is come ye might remember them that I tolde you so."

As expected, Tyndale was called to give an account for his teachings. The chancellor, having received reports of Tyndale's "heresy," summoned him to appear in his chambers. On his way to that meeting, Foxe noted Tyndale's unshakable trust in the Lord as he "cried in his mind heartily to God, to give him strength fast to stand in the truth of his word."[27] Foxe recorded Tyndale's account of what transpired in the chancellor's office:

> He threatened him grievously, reviling and rating at him as though he had been a dog, and laid to his charge many things whereof no accuser yet could be brought forth (as commonly their manner is, not to bring forth the accuser), notwithstanding that the priests of the country the same time were there present. And thus Master Tyndale, after those examinations, escaping out of their hands, departed home, and returned to his master again.[28]

---

26   Foxe, *Acts and Monuments*, 5:116.

27   Ibid.

28   Ibid.

A Friend's Advice

Before heading home to Little Sodbury, Tyndale visited William Latimer, one of his former professors during his residency at Magdalen Hall, associated with the University of Oxford. Being friends with Cuthbert Tunstall (Bishop of London),[29] Sir Thomas More, and Desiderius Erasmus, God used Latimer, who "favoured [Tyndale] well," and was a strategic mentor and trusted adviser to him.[30] Foxe describes their meeting this way:

> Tyndale went and opened his mind upon divers questions of the Scripture: for to him he durst be bold to disclose his heart. Unto whom the doctor said, "Do you not know that the pope is very Antichrist, whom the Scripture speaketh of? But beware what you say; for if you shall be perceived to be of that opinion, it will cost you your life:" and said moreover, "I have been an officer of his; but I have given it up, and defy him and all his works."[31]

William's receptiveness to Latimer's advice was a life-changing event, one that would set a sequence that would change the course of the entire world "to the end of the age" (Matt 28:20). Tyndale knew that the consequences of violating the Constitutions of Oxford were too risky for the Walshes to maintain a relationship with him. If he remained a resident in their home, their lives would have been at stake. Tyndale knew he must depart from his beloved friends, Sir John and Lady Anne Walsh, and leave his hometown of nearly twenty-nine years.

---

29   Daniell, *William Tyndale*, 83–4.

30   Foxe, *Acts and Monuments*, 5:117; Loane, *Masters of the English Reformation*, 66.

31   Foxe, *Acts and Monuments*, 5:117.

Upon his return to Little Sodbury Manor, he met with Sir John to express his concerns for both his and the Walsh family's safety. Knowing the dangers the Walshes faced and demonstrating a higher regard for them than himself (Phil 2:1–4), Tyndale recorded their meeting, saying, "Sir, I perceive I shall not be suffered to tarry long in this country, neither shall you be able, though you would, to keep me out of the hands of the spiritualty; and also what displeasure might grow thereby to you, by keeping me, God knoweth, for which I should be right sorry."[32]

God blessed John and Anne Walsh by using them to help lay the foundation for William Tyndale to expand his network to others who, like him, might be treated as criminals because "ye and all that will live godly in Christ Iesu, must suffre persecucions" (2 Tim 3:12).

Although Lady Walsh initially questioned Tyndale about why they should trust him, they eventually became his advocates and fellow workers with the truth (3 John 1–8). The "Spirit of Jesus" that prevented the Apostle Paul from going to Bithynia (Acts 16:7) is the same One that kept Tyndale from remaining in Gloucestershire. His plans were far greater; Tyndale had to move to London, the capital city, where God would introduce him to more fellow workers in Christ. July 1523 marked the last time William Tyndale ever saw Little Sodbury, as he would now encounter new relationships, both supportive and adversarial, in the city of London.

---

32   Henry Walter, ed., *The Works of William Tyndale*, vol. 1, *Doctrinal Treatises and Introductions to Different Portions of the Holy Scriptures* (1848; repr., Edinburgh: Banner of Truth Trust, 2010), xxi.

CHAPTER 3

Tyndale's Exodus to London

So that ye fyrst knowe this, that no prophesy in the scripture
hath eny private interpretacion. For the scripture cā never
by the will of man: but wholy men of god spake as
they were moved by the wholy goost.
2 Peter 1:20–21

Perhaps the small possibility of gaining favor with Latimer's associates in London gave Tyndale the courage to overlook his mentor's sober warning about dissenters.

Tyndale recognized a fundamental flaw of Roman Catholicism—"the scriptures of God were hidden from the people's eyes."[1] The words of Romans 1:16–17 reassured him: "For I am not ashamed of the gospell of Christ, because it is the power of God unto salvacion to all that believe, namely to the iewe [Jew], ād also to the gētyle, For by it the rightewesnes which commeth of God is opened, from faythe to faythe. As it is written: The iust shall live by fayth."

Choosing to act on his best option, Tyndale left the area of his hometown. As he was departing from Little Sodbury, the manor appeared smaller as he passed through the countryside until the trees obscured his last view of the house that belonged to his beloved friends, Sir John and Lady Anne Walsh.

Traveling at a reasonable pace via horseback, Tyndale would have completed the 115-mile journey to central London in four to five days. Heading east, he held cautious optimism that his plan to translate the Bible was within the bounds of the law. Technically, "men were not

---

1   Foxe, *Acts and Monuments*, 5:118.

absolutely forbidden to translate holy Scriptures; they were forbidden to translate it of their own authority; and a hope was thus apparently held out of the possibility of some translation being produced under the sanction of the bishops."[2] With his horse's every stride, he likely prayed for the Lord's favor with Cuthbert Tunstall, the Bishop of London, whose approval was essential for his translation of the Greek Bible into English.

Riding in a horse driven carriage through the hillsides would have afforded more convenience to rehearse his Gloucestershire conversations, questions, and threats he had encountered from Roman Catholic prelates, of which he was quite conversant.

Six years later, Tyndale articulated those thoughts, asserting that the prelates

> be all agreed, to drive you from the knowledge of the scripture, and that ye shall not have the text thereof in the mother-tongue, and to keep the world still in darkness, to the intent they might sit in the consciences of the people, through vain superstition and false doctrine, to satisfy their filthy lusts, their proud ambition, and unsatiable covetousness, and to exalt their own honour above king and emperor, yea, and above God himself.[3]

Tyndale practiced his New Testament translations many times, vivid in his memory would have been John 17:17–19 where Jesus prayed to the Father: "Sanctify them ī thy trueth. Thy sayinge is verite. As thou diddest send me into the worlde, evē soo have I sent them into the worlde, And for their sakes sanctify I my silfe, thatt they also myght be

---

2   Demaus, *William Tyndale*, 86.

3   Tyndale, "The Preface of Master William Tyndale that He Made before the Five Books of Moses, Called Genesis," in *Doctrinal Treatises*, 393.

sanctified thorowe the trueth." Verses like these, along with the hard-heartedness of the prelates, motivated Tyndale to translate the New Testament into English.

With each step away from home and toward London, he was emboldened by the knowledge that people were in desperate need of God's Word. Expounding on his motives for translating the Bible into English in Tunstall's house, he recounted his turmoil in Little Sodbury and the realization that he could no longer stay there: "The priests of the country be unlearned; as God it knoweth, there are a full ignorant sort, which have seen no more Latin than that they read in their port-esses and missals, which yet many of them can scarcely read."[4]

He documented their lack of skill with the Latin language, noting how they toiled over two Latin works: Albertus's *De secretis muli-erum*, copiously making "notes therein, and all to teach the midwives, as they say; and Linwode, a book of constitutions, to gather tythes, mortuaries, offerings, customs, and other pillage, which they call not theirs, but God's part, and the duty of holy church, to discharge their consciences withal."[5]

Tyndale emphasized that neither Albertus's *De secretis muli-erum* nor Linwode's book about constitutions held the authority of Scripture; those were merely human philosophies and man-made laws. Thus, he pointed out the irony of their hypocrisy, "because they are thus unlearned, thought I, when they come together to the ale-house, which is their preaching-place, they affirm that my sayings are heresy."[6]

---

4   Tyndale, "Preface to the Five Books of Moses," in *Doctrinal Treatises*, 394.

5   Tyndale, "Preface to the Five Books of Moses," in *Doctrinal Treatises*, 394. On the work *De secretis mulierum*, the title, translated into English, is *The Woman's Secrets*, written by Albertus Magnus (died November 15, 1280). Albertus Magnus, *De Secretis Mulierum: Or, the Mysteries of Human Generation Fully Revealed*, trans. John Quincy (London: E. Curll, 1725), xi.

6   Tyndale, "Preface to the Five Books of Moses," in *Doctrinal Treatises*, 394.

Common People Taken Captive

Tyndale's primary concern became the common people who were taken captive by the clergy's devotion to books that contradicted Scripture. Undoubtedly, Tyndale, along with John and Anne Walsh and Latimer, prayed for the Lord to provide them with the living Word of God so that His future redeemed people would be equipped to discern philosophical errors, just as Paul describes in Colossians 2:8–10:

> Beware lest eny mā come ād spoyle you thorowe philosophy and disceatfull vanitie, thorowe the tradiciōs of mē, ād ordinaciōs after the worlde, and not after Christ. For in hī dwelleth all the fulnes of the godheed boddyly, ād ye are full in hī, which is the heed of all rule and power.

Additionally, Tyndale's support network in Gloucestershire likely prayed for the Lord to raise up men and women who would be responsible for each of their own links connected to the larger supply chain to ensure that those villagers received a Bible.

As he journeyed to London, thoughts of Erasmus and Tunstall crossed his mind. With a touch of sarcasm, he reflected,

> As I this thought, the bishop of London came to my remembrance, whom Erasmus (whose tongue maketh of little gnats great elephants, and lifteth up above the stars whosoever giveth him a little exhibition,) praiseth exceedingly, among other, in his Annotations on the New Testament, for his great learning.[7]

---

7   Tyndale, "Preface to the Five Books of Moses," in *Doctrinal Treatises*, 395.

Despite his reservations, Tyndale valued the relationship between Erasmus and Tunstall, believing that their shared acquaintance with men like William Latimer could expedite the translation approval process. He prayed that God would providentially connect him with such men so that the "boy that driveth the plough" would know more of God's Word than the pope, highlighting the crucial role his accomplices played in implementing the plan.

As Tyndale observed the plowboys in the fields on his journey to London, did he rehearse their dilemma? Recognizing the necessity to combat false teachers with exegetically sound and hermeneutically accurate principles, Tyndale

> perceived by experience how that it was impossible to establish the lay people in any truth, except the scripture were plainly laid before their eyes and their mother tongue, that they might see the process, the order, and meaning of the text: four else whatsoever truth is taught them, these enemies of all truth quench it again, partly with the smoke of their bottomless pit whereof thou reddest apocalypse ix [Revelation 9]. that is, with apparent reason of sophistry, and traditions of their own making, founded without ground of scripture, and partly and juggling with the text, expounding it in such a sense as impossible to gather of the text, if thou see the process, order, and meaning thereof.[8]

There was an urgent need for individuals to see and understand Scripture. Providing it for them in their familiar tongue would meet that basic need and, in turn, set the churches to function as they were designed. Saints within local churches desperately needed biblically

8   Tyndale, "Preface to the Five Books of Moses," in *Doctrinal Treatises*, 394.

qualified pastors and elders (1 Tim 3:1–7; Titus 1:5–9) to train the saints to do the work of the ministry (Eph 4:11–16).

His roadside meditations and eager thoughts during his trip to London to meet Tunstall refreshed him for the next leg of his journey. He writes, "If I might come to this man's service, I were happy."[9] He needed a job, and a place to call home. Given that "Tunstall had helped Erasmus with the second edition of his Greek New Testament"[10] in 1516–17, Tyndale was optimistic that the bishop might allow him to translate the Bible in his residence.

Gaining New Adversaries and Friends in London

While in Gloucestershire, the Lord provided acquaintances who wisely advised him about how to approach the Bishop of London, Cuthbert Tunstall. Tyndale recounts, "I gat me to London, and, through the acquaintance of my master, came to sir Harry Gilford, the king's grace's comptroller."[11] Hoping to demonstrate his language expertise and to secure an appointment with Tunstall, Tyndale brought a sample of his Greek-to-English translation titled *Oration of Isocrates* which he presented to Harry Gilford.

Impressed by Tyndale's work, Gilford suggested that Tyndale write a letter to Tunstall describing the nature of his visit. When Tyndale delivered that letter, to his surprise, Tunstall's servant, William Hebilthwayte, an old acquaintance of Tyndale's, greeted him and accepted the letter on Tunstall's behalf. Initially, a reconnection seemed promising, but as Tyndale noted, the Lord had a much different plan: "God (which knoweth what is within hypocrites) saw that I was beguiled, and that that counsel was not the next way unto my purpose. And therefore he

---

9   Tyndale, "Preface to the Five Books of Moses," in *Doctrinal Treatises*, 394.

10   Daniell, *William Tyndale*, 84.

11   Tyndale, "Preface to the Five Books of Moses," in *Doctrinal Treatises*, 395.

gat me no favour in my lord's sight."[12] Although Hebilthwayte's rejection was disappointing after Tyndale's long journey, it was short-lived.

Tyndale Presses On as a Preacher

While waiting for his long-anticipated meeting with Tunstall, he served the saints by preaching God's Word at St. Dunstan's in the West. In the Lord's kindness, He brought a wealthy man named Humphrey Monmouth into his life. Humphrey was motivated to make a three-mile round trip from his home church of All Hallows, Barking, located one block west of the Tower of London, to hear Tyndale exposit God's Word. When he learned that Tyndale did not have a place to live, Monmouth invited him to lodge at his own home while he awaited his meeting with Tunstall.[13]

Though William Tyndale was an exceptional linguist "whose scholarly understanding of the implications of the new learning for the expression of the word of God was founded at Magdalen hall,"[14] Tunstall was educated at Cambridge University, and his position as the Bishop of London was more than merely a prestigious religious role; his job required entertainment, meetings and events with ambassadors, noblemen, and representing King Henry VIII in his absence.[15] Tunstall commanded and received great respect, and his acceptance of a meeting with someone like Tyndale from Gloucestershire was a rare honor, typically reserved for when he had nothing else of substance on his calendar.

---

12   Tyndale, "Preface to the Five Books of Moses," in *Doctrinal Treatises*, 395–96.

13   John Strype, *Ecclesiastical Memorials, Relating Chiefly to Religion, and the Reformation of It, and the Emergencies of the Church of England, under King Henry VIII, King Edward VI, and Queen Mary I*, vol. 1, pt. 2 (Oxford: Clarendon Press, 1822), 364.

14   Daniell, *William Tyndale*, 23.

15   Demaus, *William Tyndale*, 77.

Tyndale Meets with Tunstall

Nevertheless, at God's appointed time, Tyndale entered into the presence of the Bishop of London. There, he respectfully bowed before his superior. The bishop had known Tyndale only through his introductory epistle and translation of the *Oration of Isocrates*, a scholarly work. Yet for a man of Tunstall's education, Tyndale's accomplishments seemed comparable with many other scholars on his staff. Tyndale recounted the outcome of the meeting: "Whereupon my lord answered me, his house was full; he had more than he could well find; and advised me to seek in London, where he said I could not lack a service."[16]

With this abrupt dismissal, Tyndale did not give up hope or retreat back to Little Sodbury. Instead, he remained in London for nearly a year, living in Monmouth's home and observing how preachers relished their positions of authority. He noted their failed attempts "to set peace and unity in the world, (though it be not possible for them that walk in darkness to continue long in peace, for they cannot but either stumble or dash themselves at one thing or another that shall clean unquiet all together)."[17]

Tyndale concluded that not only was there "no room in my lord of London's palace to translate the new Testament, but also that there was no place to do it in all England, as experience doth now openly declare."[18] Nearly six years later, on January 17, 1530, William published his frustrations in the preface to his translation of the Pentateuch, discussing his determination to continue his translation work while also expressing his unflattering views of Roman Catholic prelates:

---

16   Tyndale, "Preface to the Five Books of Moses," in *Doctrinal Treatises*, 396.

17   Ibid.

18   Ibid.

What protestation should I make in such a matter unto our prelates, those stubborn Nimrods which so mightily fight against God, and resist his Holy Spirit, enforcing with all craft and subtlety to quench the light of the everlasting testament, promises, and appointment made between God and us, and heaping the fierce wrath of God upon all princes and rulers; mocking them with false feigned names of hypocrisy, and serving their lusts at all points, and dispensing with them even of the very laws of God, of which Christ himself testifieth, Matt. 5, that "not so much as one tittle thereof may perish, or be broken."[19]

Glancing back to 1523, during his time in London, the Lord prepared William Tyndale for Tunstall's rejection by shaping his pastoral experience at St. Dunstan's in the West. As he spent more time in London, Tyndale focused on translating, preaching, and building networks of people. The connections were numerous, including the church's Rector, Thomas Green, MA, whom Tyndale may have known from his time at Oxford or Cambridge.[20] Green was also associated with Thomas Poyntz, a key accomplice of Tyndale's (discussed further in chapter 9). Poyntz, a member of the Grocers' Company, likely knew Monmouth, suggesting that he may also have introduced Green to Tyndale.[21] Additionally, Thomas Poyntz was related to Sir John Walsh's first wife, Anne Poyntz-Walsh.[22] It is possible that the Walsh family contacted Thomas Green to invite Tyndale to preach at the church and to encourage Monmouth to attend.

---

19   Tyndale, "Preface to the Five Books of Moses," in *Doctrinal Treatises*, 396.

20   Daniell, *William Tyndale*, 104.

21   Mozley, *William Tyndale*, 45.

22   Sr. John Walsh of Little Sodbury was "married at one time to the daughter of Sir Robert Poyntz." Buxton, *At the House of Thomas Poyntz*, 24.

As the next chapter reveals, the relationship between Tyndale and Monmouth played a crucial role in the production and distribution of English Bibles. In London, Humphrey provided Tyndale with generous lodging accommodation and a place at his table, which was instrumental to his network building. Here, Tyndale broke bread with Monmouth's closest fellow church members and business associates—individuals who later became his accomplices, risking their necks in England and beyond the sea so that God's people could read their own copy of the Bible. While Tyndale's hopes of gaining the approval of a prominent figure to support his translation efforts were dashed, God was redeeming his time in England to support the translation work and to establish a vast network of people to play a role in its distribution.

CHAPTER 4

Monmouth Steps In to Support Tyndale

I Therfore which am ī bondes for the lordes sake exhorte you,
thatt ye walke worthy off the vocation wher with ye are called.
Ephesians 4:1

Shortly after William's arrival in London in 1523, the Lord singled out Humphrey Monmouth, a businessman, from its 50,000 residents to help Tyndale supply His inerrant Word to the English-speaking world. Monmouth was much more than an eager listener of Tyndale's sermons and a gracious host who provided a safe space during growing hostility towards those who challenged the status quo. God uniquely gifted and positioned this accomplished individual to fund and facilitate support from his vast network of associates.

Though the exact date of his birth is unknown, he likely was born between 1482 and 1487, and he died between the ages of 50 and 55 on November 23, 1537.[1]

The surname "Monmouth" could be linked to the Monmouth area, located west of the River Severn, which borders England and Wales. The name was common in the town of Tewkesbury, and it was the title of the Prior of Monmouth in Longhope, both situated in Gloucestershire.[2] While this does not definitively connect Humphrey

---

1   Humphrey Monmouth dates his will on November 16, 1537. Strype, *Ecclesiastical Memorials,* 368. Andrew Hope reports that Monmouth died one week later, placing the date of his death on November 23, 1537. Andrew Hope, "Thomas More and Humphrey Monmouth: Conscience and Coercion in Reformation England," in *Theorizing Legal Personhood in Late Medieval England,* ed. Andreea D. Boboc, Medieval Law and Its Practice 18 (Leiden: Brill, 2015), 259.

2   Hoyle, *Military Survey of Gloucestershire,* 164, 206.

to specific families, he most likely shared ancestral roots in the general vicinity of Monmouth and Monmouthshire.

Biographer David Daniell suggests that Humphrey probably came from Gloucestershire.[3] Furthermore, Robert Demaus notes that "it is not impossible that he [Monmouth] may have known something of Tyndale's family, or may have had business connections with them; for he probably came from the county of Monmouth, close to Tyndale's birthplace; his brother settled in Worcestershire, and Tyndale's relations were engaged in the cloth manufacture in Gloucestershire."[4]

Scripture Man

Apparently, Tyndale's sermons and translations did not introduce the gospel to Monmouth. According to John Foxe, in the years leading up to 1512, Monmouth "began to smell the gospel,"[5] indicating he was already familiar with and receptive to Tyndale's work. He was a known "Lollard," adhering to the Reformed teaching of John Wycliffe and furthermore referred to as "Scripture Man." Both monikers originated as derisive terms that referenced those who read and preached from John Wycliffe's English translation of Jerome's Latin Vulgate Bible, which was already 1,100 years old.

"Scripture Man" became one of William Tyndale's first accomplices in London. From the prosperity of Monmouth's multinational business interests, the Lord blessed Tyndale with a safe place to live and to interact with his landlord's well-connected supply chain partners. These influential and widespread relationships proved vital to the distribution of English Bibles extending their reach beyond "the plough boy" in Gloucester. In the home of Humphrey Monmouth, Tyndale continued

---

3   Daniell, *William Tyndale*, 104.

4   Demaus, *William Tyndale*, 74.

5   Foxe, *Acts and Monuments*, 4:618.

to prepare the sermons he preached at St. Dunstan's Church in the West. There, most importantly, he refined his translations of the Greek New Testament, which were the foundations for the printing and mass distribution of the English Bible.

Doer of the Word

The Lord's preparation of Monmouth enabled him to effectively manage his successful commercial enterprises and relationships in order to facilitate the translation, printing, smuggling, and distribution of English Bibles throughout England, Wales, and Scotland. When examining the life and testimony of Humphrey Monmouth, one should consider how the scent of the gospel gladly compelled him to be a doer of the Word, and not just a hearer only (James 1:22). As one who smelled the gospel, Monmouth stewarded his God-given talents, gifts, and resources to advance the Great Commission.[6]

A Man of the Cloth

The earliest records show that Humphrey Monmouth was a cloth merchant associated with the Drapers' Company, serving as an apprentice from 1495 to 1503 under the mentorship of Edmund Burges.[7] After completing his eight-year apprenticeship at around the age of twenty, he was granted "Admission to the Freedom by Apprenticeship"

---

6   For a deeper study about stewarding the Lord's resources towards the Great Commission, see Eric Weathers, "Shrewdly Investing in the Great Commission: The Parable in Luke 16:1–13," in *Biblical Missions: Principles, Priorities, Practices*, ed. Mark Tatlock and Chris Burnett (Nashville: Thomas Nelson, 2025), 319–25.

7   Penny Fussell to Eric Weathers, email, May 20, 2025, Drapers' Company Archives, London. "I can confirm that Humphrey Monmouth was a Draper. In the early 20th century a member called Percival Boyd created a register of past apprentices and Freemen. Taking information from the Company's archives (such as accounts and membership registers) as well as occasionally including information form external printed sources (such as wills), Boyd arranged the register in date order within family group names. The register is called Boyd's Roll. Attached is the extract for Monmouth."

in 1503,[8] which allowed him to operate his own trade business under the regulations of the Drapers' Company. He eventually became known as "a great dealer in Suffolk cloths."[9] Monmouth continued to rise within the ranks of the Drapers' Company. In 1507, he was awarded an elite position of "Livery of the Company," and he held an annual position of "Warden" for four years, all within the 1519 to 1532 timeframe.

In 1535 (the same year that Tyndale was arrested in Antwerp), Monmouth was elected as Sheriff/Alderman.[10] In 1536 (the year that Tyndale was executed), he was elected to the most prestigious position within the Drapers' Company, taking on the role of "Master."[11] Monmouth's industry was significant in England; in fact, "no other industry created more employment or generated more wealth. As many as 1 in 7 of the country's workforce were probably making cloth and 1 in 4 households were involved in spinning."[12] Monmouth was able to use the success of the industry as well as his influence over it as leverage in 1529, when he was in a great deal of trouble and the King's economic viability was stretched by threats of war and widespread unemployment.

As a member and administrator of this prestigious livery company, Monmouth enjoyed considerable advantages. The Drapers' Company had "a clear hierarchy, with wardens, masters and other officers, a governing court that regulated the activities of members and disciplined those who broke the company's rules and laws, a hall for common feasting the (social life of any company was hugely important)

---

8   Fussell to Weathers, May 20, 2025.

9   John Strype, *Ecclesiastical Memorials, Relating Chiefly to Religion and the Reformation of It, and the Emergencies of the Church of England, under King Henry VIII, King Edward VI, and Queen Mary I,* vol. 1, pt. 1 (Oxford: Clarendon Press, 1822), 487.

10   Fussell to Weathers, May 20, 2025.

11   Ibid.

12   John S. Lee, *"Working in the Middle Ages: The Medieval Clothier,"* Medievalists.net, September 2018, accessed August 20, 2025, https://www.medievalists.net/2018/09/working-in-the-middle-ages-the-medieval-clothier/.

and often a Chapel for worship."[13] Also known as "The Worshipful Company of Drapers," his membership facilitated numerous business connections across London's top livery companies. These relationships ultimately brought trusted individuals to assist Tyndale. Though they did not know it prior to arriving for Sunday services at St. Dunstan's in the West in 1523, it became clear to Tyndale and Monmouth that God set an appointment for them to meet one another shortly after Tyndale finished his sermon.

The Parable of the Rich Man and the Poor Man

Monmouth's reputation as a "Scripture Man" may have originated from a close friend, Hugh Latimer, who referred to him in a sermon on Romans 12:20–21 that he preached in 1555.[14] John Foxe wrote about Latimer's sermon illustration, which served as a parable depicting Monmouth as a godly wealthy man who showed love to his impoverished neighbor by providing financial resources and fellowship at his table when the neighbor was hungry. Foxe notes that Latimer's illustration dates back several years, to a time "when Dr. Colet was in trouble, and should have been burned, if God had not turned the King's heart to the contrary."[15] Since Colet was tried for heresy around 1512, this suggests that Monmouth began to be known as "Scripture Man" around that time.

In Latimer's parable, Monmouth and the poor man sat at the dinner table, discussing the gospel. However, when Monmouth "reproved popery, and such kind of things," his guest "took great displeasure against" him. This reaction resembles the crowds in John 6, who sought free food and healing, but walked away when they finally

---

13   Stephen Alford, *London's Triumph: Merchant Adventurers and the Tudor City* (London: Bloomsbury, 2017), 3–4.

14   For an enriching study about the "Poor Man" parable, see Daniell, 104–06, and Mozley, 44.

15   Foxe, *Acts and Monuments*, 4:618.

understood Jesus' preaching of the gospel (John 6:60–66). For them, Jesus' message was not as valuable as the complimentary groceries or free medical care. Similarly, the poor man, filled with resentment towards Monmouth, rejected both financial assistance and the opportunity to eat at his table. Unaware of the man's anger, Monmouth continued to seek conversations with him, but to no avail. When they crossed paths on the street, the poor man avoided confrontation and walked away. Eventually, they met on a narrow road, as the poor man tried to escape, Monmouth grabbed his hand, looked him in the eyes, and asked, "Neighbor! What is come into your heart to take such displeasure with me? What have I done against you? Tell me, and I will be ready at all times to make you amends." Latimer continues the parable, explaining, "He spake so gently, so charitably, so lovingly and friendly, that it wrought so in the poor man's heart, that by and by he fell down upon his knees and asked him forgiveness." With forgiveness came a reconciled friendship, "and they loved as well as ever they did before."[16]

Humphrey Monmouth's reconciliation demonstrates that he was a blessed man for having shown mercy towards the poor man, all from a pure heart. Striving for peace with the man showed that God blessed him as a peacemaker and a son of God (Matt 5:7–9). Monmouth's status as a Freeman in the Drapers' Company was also a great blessing, affording him privileges bestowed on few in the early sixteenth century. However, his wealth and societal position did not exempt him from the king's laws, particularly those forbidding the ownership and reading of the Bible in any language. As his desire grew for the scent of the gospel, Monmouth, like a man named Richard Hunne, experienced hostility directed toward those who live a godly life.

---

16   Foxe, *Acts and Monuments*, 4:619.

The Cloaked Murder of Richard Hunne

The extent to which Roman Catholic authorities expressed hostility was boundless, including murder disguised as suicide. A notable example is Richard Hunne (Hun), whose story is detailed in John Foxe's twenty-two-page account about those who conspired to kill him in 1514.[17] Foxe recounts that after the death of Hunne's 5-week-old son, the parish clerk demanded that he return the boy's "bearing sheet" to cover mortuary fees. Grieving the loss of his son, Hunne found this demand insulting and refused to comply. The two parties sued and countersued, but when the rest of the priestly order learned of the situation, they were outraged that a layman would dare to sue them. They determined that such a precedent must not be allowed. Foxe reports that the prelates conspired "to entrap and bring him within the danger of their own cruel laws." As a known "Lollard," Richard Hunne was accused of heresy and imprisoned in the "Lollards' Tower" at St. Paul's Cathedral. Shortly thereafter, he was found hanging with a rope around his neck.[18]

Foxe provides detailed testimony suggesting that Hunne's death was thought to be suicide; however, in light of incontrovertible evidence, the court later dismissed this claim. Following a coroner's inquest and widespread public outrage, the court concluded that three church officials had conspired to kill Hunne and subsequently found them guilty of murder. Undeterred, the Roman Catholic governing authorities posthumously convicted Hunne of heresy (as reported by Foxe), leaving his family impoverished.[19] They exhumed his body and burned his remains at Smithfield shortly after his death in December 1514.

As contemporaries, it is likely that Monmouth was acquainted with Hunne, who was a Christian, a successful businessman, and a member

---

17   Foxe, *Acts and Monuments*, 4:183–205.

18   Ibid., 4:185.

19   Stephen Inwood, *A History of London* (London: Macmillan, 1998), 149.

of the Merchant Taylors' Company. Even if Monmouth did not know him personally, he would have certainly taken notice of Hunne's infamous case. Stephen Inman notes that "in the years following the Hunne case, anti-clerical feelings were intensified by the career of Thomas Wolsey, Cardinal, Archbishop of York, and Lord Chancellor from 1515 to 1529, who personified all the vices Colet condemned—pride, wealth, ambition, temporal power and worldly morality—in their most extreme form."[20] It is no wonder that Tyndale dubbed Cardinal Wolsey Cardinal "Wolfsee."[21] The mistreatment of Hunne by the Roman Catholic church authorities must have alerted Monmouth of the need to advance the gospel wisely, especially in light of the imminent threats of persecution for years to come.

The Freedom of a Christian

In 1520, Martin Luther wrote a book with a greeting to "The Perceptive, wise Hieronymus Mühlpfort," administrator of the town of Zwickau, titled *De Libertate Christiana* [The freedom of a Christian]. Although written in German, Luther composed a Latin version directed at Pope Leo X, aiming for a much broader audience "so that for everyone my teaching and writing on the papacy will appear based on something for which I could not be reproached."[22] Monmouth testified in his 1529 deposition that he owned a copy of this book. Moreover, this work played a crucial role in Monmouth's desire for reformation in England. John Strype noted, "this man, when Luther's doctrine came first into England, was an embracer of it, and conversed much in his writings, and did what he could for the enlarging and spreading evangelical knowledge therein contained."[23]

---

20   Inwood, *History of London*, 149.

21   Tyndale, "The Obedience of a Christian Man," in *Expositions and Notes*, 310.

22   Martin Luther, *The Freedom of a Christian*, trans. Robert Kolb (Wheaton, IL: Crossway, 2023), 28–29.

23   Strype, *Ecclesiastical Memorials*, vol. 1, pt. 1, 487–88.

In 1521, Roman Catholic authorities added *De Libertate Christiana* to their list of forbidden books. However, having learned from Richard Hunne's fate, Monmouth, a savvy businessman and strategic thinker, advanced the English Reformation by concealing some of these banned books in plain sight. According to Sir Thomas More's articles against him, Monmouth was implicated in 1528 with the claim "that the book *De Libertate Christiana* was written in the beginning, and drawn out of St. Augustine's works, and the Exposition of the *Pater Noster* was ascribed to Hilarius, to blynd and abuse thereby your readers of them, as they were books of holly Fathers."[24] Monmouth's strategy was shrewd; he concealed *De Libertate Christiana* within the cover of a book by St. Augustine and hid the *Exposition of the Pater Noster* inside a work by Hilarius, which was a "commentary [that] was very possibly of Lollard origin."[25] More argued that Monmouth disguised these books to make readers believe they were authored by Roman Catholic theologians. Together, these two texts reveal crucial information about how Monmouth advanced from his *smelling of the gospel* in 1512 to a deeper understanding of the gospel in 1521.[26] His appreciation of the themes in these works demonstrate how the Lord strengthened his faith by rooting him in Scripture.

From *De Libertate Christiana*, we learn that Luther's writing emboldened Monmouth to place his trust in the Word of God. Luther's two theses promote evangelism of unbelievers, encourage believers, and challenge the oppressive religious norms of his era. Based on 1 Corinthians 9:19, and Romans 13:8, his first thesis declares, "a Christian is a free lord of everything and subject to no one." While the second states, "a Christian is a willing servant of everything and subject to everyone."[27]

---

24 Strype, *Ecclesiastical Memorials*, vol. 1, pt. 1, 489.
25 Hope, "Thomas More and Humphrey Monmouth," 251.
26 Cf. Foxe, *Acts and Monuments*, 4:618.
27 Luther, *Freedom of a Christian*, 29.

Reflecting on Luther's remarks regarding garments worn by religious leaders, Monmouth recognized that, "it does not help the soul at all if the body wears holy garments, as priests and others in holy orders do, nor does it help if the body is inside the church or in some holy places."[28] As he continued reading, Monmouth was captivated by Luther's clear expositions of Scripture. Surely, he rejoiced over Luther's treatment of John 11:25, where Jesus says that He is the resurrection and the life, and that whoever believes in Him will live eternally, even if he dies. He was equally moved by Luther's comments on John 14:6, leaving him in awe of Jesus' bold proclamation: "I am the way the truth and the life, no one comes to the Father but through Me." From Luther's writings, Monmouth found no instructions about keeping Roman Catholic sacraments and nothing about eating meat during Lent. Likewise, he found no descriptions of works being required for salvation nor mentions about pilgrimages to Rome being profitable for the soul.[29]

Additionally, Monmouth's scent for the gospel became more acute as he savored Luther's treatment of Matthew 4:4: "a person does not live on bread alone but on every word that comes forth from the mouth of God."[30] After contemplating Luther's assertion that "we must be assured that the soul can get along without everything except God's word, and it finds no help in anything apart from God's word. But when it has the word it needs nothing else,"[31] Monmouth undoubtedly bowed his head in prayer, pleading with the Father to provide him and all people with printed copies of His inspired Word "that the man of god maye be perfet, and prepared unto all good works" (2 Tim 3:17).

---

28 Luther, *Freedom of a Christian*, 39.

29 These are just a sampling of the articles leveled against Monmouth. For further details, see Strype, *Ecclesiastical Memorials*, vol. 1, pt. 1, 488–492.

30 Luther, *Freedom of a Christian*, 33.

31 Ibid.

Out of desperation, he must have prayed, "but Lord, who will trans-late the Bible into my language?" Unbeknownst to him, three years later, the Lord would bring a premiere Oxford Greek scholar, William Tyndale, into his life. It had only been a year since Monmouth welcomed William into his home, following the publication of Erasmus's 1522 edition of the Greek New Testament. This same edition was used by Tyndale while living in Monmouth's home from late 1523 to around April 1524, serving as the foundation for completing the first English translation of the Bible by the end of 1525.[32]

Preparing for Tyndale's Exile to Europe

When Tyndale realized that he would never receive permission to translate the Bible into English, he knew that he could no longer stay at his beloved friend's house—neither could he stay in London or even England as a whole—he began planning his exodus to a place where he could translate the Bible into English from the original languages.[33]

At the time of Tyndale's departure, Monmouth held one of four prestigious positions as a Warden of the Drapers' Company.[34] He had the skill, wisdom, network, and the financial means to help smuggle Bibles into England. Humphrey promised Tyndale £10 sterling for praying "for his father's and mother's souls, and all Christian souls; which money afterwards he sent him over to Hamburgh, according to his promise."[35] Monmouth's commitment to underwrite Tyndale's cost of living, translation efforts, travel expenses, and books meant they worked shoulder-to-shoulder, even while hundreds of miles apart.

---

32 "No Greek Testament was in reality accessible to him, except that of Erasmus, which had been origi-nally printed in 1516, and of which a second edition appeared in 1519, and a third in 1522. From this third edition of Erasmus it can be demonstrated that Tyndale made his English version." Demaus, *William Tyndale*, 99.

33 Tyndale, "Preface to the Five Books of Moses," *Doctrinal Treatises*, 396.

34 Fussell to Weathers, May 20, 2025.

35 Foxe, *Acts and Monuments*, 4:618.

Robert Demaus records in his biography of William Tyndale that £10 sterling was "probably a hundred pounds" in his day (1871).[36] To put that in perspective, £100 sterling in 1871 is worth £15,052.88 in the year 2025.[37] Additionally, he financially supported and encouraged, "the translation of the holy Scriptures into English, and contributed largely both to the translating and printing of them.... He also assisted in the printing of books in English beyond sea."[38]

Further, Monmouth already held significant contracts with shipping companies importing his goods on a massive scale; he had close contacts with German merchants in London who worked at the Steelyard, stealthily circulating reformers' books and tracks smuggled in from the low countries. The London Steelyard was situated on the banks of the River Thames, just upstream from London Bridge, serving as the local headquarters for the German Hanseatic League. This League represented merchant organizations and facilitated trade between England and nearly 200 cities in Northern Europe. Owned by Germans, the Steelyard included numerous business and residential buildings. Although the Steelyard featured a chapel, many German employees chose to attend services at the nearby Allhallows the Great.[39] Monmouth engaged with Reformed Steelyard workers from various cities in the low countries who had successfully smuggled Luther's Reformed writings from Germany into England. His connections included trade negotiators, clerks, accountants, weighers, inspectors, and administrators—names that may be forgotten, just like William

---

36   Demaus, *William Tyndale*, 83.

37   Ian Webster, "Value of 1871 British Pounds Today | UK Inflation Calculator," in2013dollars.com, last modified April 24, 2025, https://www.in2013dollars.com/uk/inflation/1871. According to XE, £15,052.88 on October 7, 2025, was worth $20,233.07 US dollars. "Currency Converter: GBP to USD," XE.com, accessed October 7, 2025, https://www.xe.com/currencyconverter/convert/?Amount=15052.88&From=GBP&To=USD.

38   Strype, *Ecclesiastical Memorials*, vol. 1, pt. 1, 488.

39   Philippe Dollinger, *The German Hansa*, trans. D. S. Ayalon and S. H. Winston (Stanford, CA: Stanford University Press, 1970), 102.

Tyndale and Humphrey Monmouth—who risked their lives to deliver God's Word to the people of England in the spring of 1526 and beyond. As an expert importer, Monmouth likely brought Bibles through Welsh ports and then through entry points in Bristol where there was a "lack of royal customs officers," making it especially difficult to intercept smuggling of most imported products.[40] The English port in Bristol was particularly advantageous, and through it many forbidden books were likely delivered and distributed to Reformed leaning students and faculty at the nearby University of Oxford.

It was God who appointed Monmouth to steward his business expertise and his extensive network of friends and multinational associates from England to the low countries, extending into Germany. All this was God's answer to Humphrey's cry for Scripture "which is able to make the wyse unto health throwe fayth, which ys in Christ Iesu" (2 Tim 3:15), to be accessible to the English speaking world. Had Tyndale remained within the king's realm, the full force of the Constitutions of Oxford would have been leveled against him. Tyndale seemed to be the only man in the sixteenth century that had the heart, love for the Lord, courage and the skill to translate the Greek and Hebrew Bible into English. As he assessed the situation, he determined that he must quietly go into exile. Mozley writes of Tyndale's departure, saying, he "went forth into exile, bidding his last farewell to his native land, the first of a long line of English reformers to seek refuge abroad. He was content to be without his country, that he might serve his country."[41]

As Tyndale embarked on a three-week journey from London, crossing the North Sea to the Elba River on his way to Hamburg, Germany, there is no evidence that his accomplice, Humphrey Monmouth, ever saw him again on this side of Heaven. Nevertheless, Monmouth

---

40   Evan T. Jones, *Inside the Illicit Economy: Reconstructing the Smugglers' Trade of Sixteenth Century Bristol* (London: Routledge, 2016), 47.

41   Mozley, *William Tyndale*, 49.

continued to be his fellow worker with the truth (3 John 8). As we will explore, his commitment to the Lord came at a considerable personal cost. His courageous actions not only led to his imprisonment in the Tower of London, but also considerable economic hardship for cloth workers and the nation as a whole.

Progress and Setbacks in Germany

Derely beloved thou doest faythfully whatt soever thou
doest to the brethren, and to straungers, which bare witnes off
thy love before all the congregacion. Which brethren when thou
bryngest forwardes on their iorney (as it besemet God) thou shalt
do wele: be cause that for his names sake they went forth, and toke
no thynge of the gentyls. We therfore ought to receave soche,
that we also myght be helpers to the trueth.
3 John 5–8

I t is unlikely that Tyndale's accomplices were familiar with 3 John,
if they even knew anything about it at all. This short letter, written
to a certain Gaius, is a prime example of a faithful Christian using his
resources to support the work of missions.[1] The Apostle John compli-
mented Gaius for his devoted love and support of missionaries—likely
evangelists—whom he had not previously met, but who were probably
commissioned by the church of Ephesus. In verse 6, John encourages
Gaius with these words: "you will do well to send them on their way in
a manner worthy of God."

Before William Tyndale departed from London, Humphrey
Monmouth and his network of "certain other good men" provided
Tyndale with the financial resources necessary for his three-week,
550-nautical-mile journey by ship to Hamburg, Germany.[2] They
ensured that he had the financial means to study Hebrew for nearly
a year in Wittenberg, which was crucial for making his translation of

---

1   Eric Weathers, "Holding the Rope: 3 John for Missions Donors," 345.
2   Foxe, *Acts and Monuments*, 5:118.

59

Genesis through Deuteronomy. For these patrons, supporting Tyndale's living expenses was a nation-changing investment. Like Gaius, they were his "fellow workers with the truth" (3 John 8), working shoulder-to-shoulder from over 600-miles away because they, and their fellow citizens, were famished for the Word of God in their own language.

Monmouth's business connections with known Reformed German merchants[3] at London's Steelyard (located less than a mile between Monmouth's home in All Hallows, Barking, and the church where Tyndale preached, St. Dunstan's in the West) provided Tyndale with a Hamburg contact—a widow named Margaret von Emerson. Her husband, John, had passed away at least two years prior, leaving her with raising six children on a limited budget.[4] Like Gaius, she continued "walking in the truth" (3 John 3). Her dependance upon God's sovereignty compelled her to act faithfully in whatever she accomplished. All her endeavors, and her love for God's people, brought great joy in serving those in Christ, especially a stranger like William Tyndale (3 John 4–5). The Lord orchestrated for this courageous widow to become Tyndale's next accomplice. By stewarding her resources for God's glory, she provided room and board to travel-weary William Tyndale for a few days before continuing his journey to Wittenberg, but this would not be the last instance of Margaret serving William Tyndale for the sake of Christ.

Though Monmouth promised £10 sterling to Tyndale upon his arrival in Germany, he would not receive these funds for nearly a year. He may have carried another £10 donated by "merchants who thought the New Testament would prove a profitable article of trade in England,"[5] suggesting that the economic value of English Bibles

---

3   It is likely that Martin Luther's *De libertate Christiana*, *The Freedom of a Christian*, which he wrote for the pope, were distributed through their hands starting around 1520.

4   Mozley, *William Tyndale*, 152.

5   Ibid., 48.

was a risky yet wise investment for sixteenth-century venture capitalists familiar with the principles of supply and demand. Regardless, it is clear that Tyndale had substantial help from others who pleaded with the Lord for their own Bibles, "Affluent laics [lay people] occupied in commerce, and clerics dissatisfied with foreign domination over the Church in England, combined to hasten its consummation."[6]

Fame and fortune were not temptations for Tyndale or his associates; they served Christ under the threat of the 1408 Constitutions of Oxford, which put them at extreme risk for printing the English Bible. Tyndale was acutely aware of this danger, as he noted five years later in *The Practice of Prelates*: "They will suffer no man to know God's word, but burn it, and make heresy of it: yea, and because the people begin to smell their falsehood, they make it treason to the king, and breaking of the king's peace, to have so much as their Pater noster [the Lord's Prayer] in English."[7] A successful outcome relied on each individual link within the supply chain maintaining secrecy; any misstep could lead to swift persecution, torture, or death. Tyndale's arrival at the von Emerson home was quiet, and his stay was brief to avoid detection, ensuring his swift arrival in Wittenberg, a 180-mile journey from Hamburg.

The University of Wittenberg

For Tyndale, maintaining secrecy during that first year was effective, as the name "William Tyndale" does not even appear in the enrollment records for the University of Wittenberg. Many other names are listed, including that of a close associate, William Roye, who is also from London. His name is recorded in the university registry on June 10, 1525—nearly a year after Tyndale was believed to have arrived

---

6   Kingdon, *Incidents in the Lives*, 11.
7   Tyndale, "Obedience of a Christian Man," in *Doctrinal Treatises*, 243.

at the university.[8] Mozley was famous for his exhaustive study of the University of Wittenberg's student enrollment records. He painstakingly combed through documents, concluding that the name "William Tyndale" was indeed absent. Could it be that both Tyndale's ardent supporters and nemeses alike were misled into thinking he was in Wittenberg for almost a year? Have historians since 1524 misunderstood or misremembered Tyndale's studies at the University with Martin Luther and Philip Melanchthon?

Mozley turned the enrollment pages back to May 30, 1524, and was astonished to find a familiar name: "Mathias von Emerson," the nephew of the faithful widow Margaret. Mathias was the son of Mathias von Emerson Sr., a senator who had remarried the sister of a well-known yet controversial reformer named Marquard Schuldorp from Schleswig-Holstein, the northernmost state in Germany.[9] Schuldorp was Mathias von Emerson Jr.'s uncle and a former student of Martin Luther in Wittenberg in 1521.[10] As part of "one of the great Lutheran families of the town,"[11] the von Emersons had rich Reformation heritage. Piecing together the timeline reveals that just a few weeks before Matthias von Emerson Jr.'s enrollment, Tyndale stayed with his Aunt Margaret at the recommendation of Humphrey Monmouth's connections at the London Steelyard. And while it cannot be proven that William Tyndale was a student at the University of Wittenberg, evidence supports the assertion that he probably was.

---

8   Mozley, *William Tyndale*, 52.

9   Ibid., 152.

10   Carl Bertheau, "Schuldorp, Marquard," in *Allgemeine Deutsche Biographie*, vol. 32 (Leipzig: Verlag von Dunder & Humblot, 1891), 657–658.

11   Mozley, *William Tyndale*, 152.

William Daltici from England

Three days before Matthias von Emerson's enrollment on May 30, 1524, Mozley observed, "and in close neighbourhood to him, under the date May 27, stands the name *Guillelmus Daltici ex Anglia*, William Daltici from England. Who is this?" The answer to his question required further research, which led him to Dr. Reincke, then director of the Hamburg Staatsarchiv [State Archives], "who suggested to me that William Tyndale lay here concealed."[12] Mozley was baffled as to how investigators had overlooked this obscure name for the previous 100 years, something which he was, admittedly, unable to explain. At the time of his presumed enrollment, Tyndale was fluent in at least six languages, and the name Daltici did not resemble any of the dialects he spoke. Mozley expressed his excitement about this discovery:

> But suddenly it flashed upon me that by reversing the two syllables of *Tindal* you get *Daltin*, which only differs from *Daltici* by one letter. The present register is but a copy of the original, and if the copyist misread the final letter, all becomes clear. In those perilous times it was common enough for men to disguise their names. Robert Barnes is entered in the Wittenberg register of 1533 as *Antonius Anglus*, though his real name was added in the margin by Melanchthon.[13]

As confirmed by David Daniell, Mozley "presented an ingenious argument," but Daniell remained skeptical, "are we to think, moreover that Tyndale drank at the fountainheads of Hebrew scholarship as well

---

12   Mozley, *William Tyndale*, 53.

13   Ibid.

as Greek and German in those 'nine or ten months' in Wittenberg?"[14] It is evident that during his first year in exile from England, Wittenberg would have been the perfect place for a brilliant linguist like Tyndale to refine his knowledge of a seventh and eighth language—German and Hebrew—especially under the instruction of men like Aurogallus, a professor of Hebrew.[15]

Supplementary testimony of his tutelage under Wittenberg professors may satisfy further curiosity. John Stokesley, the Bishop of London, charged Humphrey Monmouth in 1528 for having given "exhibition to William Tyndale, Roy, and such others; for helping them over the sea to Luther; for administering privy help to translate as well the Testament and other books to English."[16] And Mozley suggests that Thomas More's writings, which claimed that Tyndale was with Luther in Wittenberg, stemmed from coercive interrogations aimed at obtaining testimony that supported his antagonistic conclusions against his adversaries; or perhaps they stemmed from strained accusations from men like John Cochlaeus, an ardent opponent of Tyndale in Cologne, Germany, in 1525 and beyond.[17]

Tyndale's Motive for Translation

The circumstantial evidence for Tyndale's presence in Wittenberg is compelling, regardless of his exact location during those months in 1524, his determination to translate the New Testament shortly after leaving Margaret von Emerson's house is evident from his own writings years later in "The Practice of Prelates." Tyndale writes of his mindset for translating the New Testament:

---

14   Daniell, *William Tyndale*, 300.
15   Mozley, *William Tyndale*, 52.
16   Foxe, *Acts and Monuments*, 4:617.
17   Daniell, *William Tyndale*, 299.

I had perceived by experience, how that it was impossible to establish the lay-people in any truth, except the scripture were plainly laid before their eyes in their mother-tongue, that they might see the process, order, and meaning of the text: for else, whatsoever truth is taught them, these enemies of all truth quench it again, partly with the smoke of their bottomless pit, whereof thou readest in Apocalypse, chap. 9 (that is, with apparent reasons of sophistry, and traditions of their own making, founded without ground of scripture,) and partly in juggling with the text, expounding it in such a sense as is impossible to gather of the text, if thou see the process, order, and meaning thereof.[18]

It was for this reason that, in the spring of 1525, Tyndale migrated 182 miles northwest, likely returning to Margaret von Emerson's house in Hamburg. About a month before this journey, he sent a letter to Humphrey Monmouth, requesting the £10 donation he had promised. Accompanying that letter, Tyndale included what Humphrey later referred to as "a little treatise."[19] Many have speculated about the nature of this treatise, but it is plausible that it was an advanced copy of the Gospel of Matthew, or at least a portion thereof, to serve as a proof source to generate excitement for the arrival of the entire English New Testament in England. Additionally, it is reasonable that Tyndale reached out to his supporters in London for further grants to cover the printing cost of 6,000 New Testaments.

---

18 Tyndale, "Preface to the Five Books of Moses," *Doctrinal Treatises*, 394.

19 Mozley, *William Tyndale*, 54.

Tyndale's Second Hamburg Layover

During this layover, another fellow-worker, Hans Collenbeeke, a merchant at the London Steelyard, delivered the funds that Monmouth had promised nearly a year earlier. At that time, Collenbeeke likely presented additional donations from other London patrons. As for Tyndale and his accomplices, their lives were on the verge of becoming increasingly complicated. His journey back to Hamburg, followed by a move to Cologne—250 miles to the southwest, necessitated a high level of confidentiality, demanding discretion of his current and future friends. Throughout the year, William Tyndale focused on refining his translation of the 1525 New Testament and enhancing his skills in Hebrew and German. In Cologne, he would meet with printers and logistics experts; they were likely recommended by Monmouth's colleagues at the London Steelyard who helped secure their loyalty to fulfill this dangerous mission.

Tyndale in Cologne, Germany

To maintain the highest level of secrecy, Tyndale chose the predominantly Roman Catholic city of Cologne to print the 1525 English New Testament, probably at the advice of his associates. Although this approach might seem counterintuitive, Tyndale selected Cologne because he believed his adversaries would search for him in predominantly Lutheran regions. This strategy suggested that it was less likely for bounty hunters to discover him in a city populated with devoted Catholics, whom they knew would willingly alert governing authorities for his printing of the New Testament.

Monmouth's financial support, along with contributions from others in his network, was in response to the Lord's favor in their lives so that they could underwrite Tyndale's living expenses and the printing of 6,000 Bibles for distribution back in England. The costs of producing English Bibles in Germany during 1525–26 remain uncertain. Typesetters arranged movable letters to create approximately 200–300 words per page. And despite their speed, Tyndale's Bible comprised about 720 pages, meaning that the time spent and attention to detail contributed to the final retail price. Brian Moynahan notes that Bibles were sold in England for an average of 3 shillings, with retail prices typically three to four times greater than production costs. He suggests that if a printer charged Tyndale 10 pence per unbound sheet, it would be reasonable to estimate the cost of printing 3,000 copies of Tyndale's New Testament at around £125.[20] William expressed the need for a faithful companion "to write, and to help me to compare the texts together."[21] Of course, an additional helper added to the cost of production, but Monmouth knew many believers from a convent in Greenwich, including a friar named William Roye, whom he likely sent to assist Tyndale in writing and comparing texts.[22]

Tyndale probably completed the translation of the 1525 English New Testament before arriving in Cologne. Speed was essential for successful execution; he could not afford to spend too much time on translation activities in Cologne and needed to complete the printing as swiftly as possible so that the Bibles could be quickly loaded on ships bound for England.

Tyndale and those who worked with him anticipated the inflated expense involved with securing an experienced, second generation printer like Peter Quentel, who was acquainted with the dangers of printing banned books. The handsome funding provided by Tyndale's accomplices allowed him to indemnify Quentel against catastrophic damages.[23]

20 Moynahan, *God's Bestseller*, 71.

21 Tyndale, "The Parable of the Wicked Mammon," in *Doctrinal Treatises*, 38.

22 Mozley, *William Tyndale*, 56.

23 Demaus, *William Tyndale*, 107.

The concern about books banned by governing authorities worked to Quentel's advantage, as he could charge premiums for undercover operations in the face of the growing risk. Embargoes on Protestant books, coupled with Catholic outrage—threats of violence and complaints from Catholic writers about the growing demand for Reformed works—raised curiosity and demand for the publications, as well as the profit from printing them. Strategically, Tyndale capitalized on this economic situation to ensure that printers, even those who were theologically opposed to the Reformation, were eager to profit from the sale of these Bibles.

Let the Printing Begin!

While the goal was to print 6,000 New Testaments, Quentel, anticipating potential mishaps or significant losses, began the first print run with 3,000. He knew that if those Bibles sold out, they could quickly print more.[24] With the contracts in place, Quentel and his staff quickly set the movable type to the milestone marker identified with the letter K,[25] now recognized as Matthew 22:12.

With everything in place, Quentel and his staff ran the presses, making history by printing the first New Testament pages in English sourced from Greek manuscripts. Even the most skilled pressman would have marveled at the wooden hinges and the corkscrew-shaped apparatus that clamped the ink-laden movable type against fresh paper. The exact number of wooden presses Quentel used to produce the 3,000 Bibles remains unknown. The commotion of the wooden machines, the sights, the sounds, and the scent of ink must have overwhelmed the

---

24   John Cochlaeus's letter to King Henry the VIII, quoted in Mozley, *William Tyndale*, 58.

25   Since William Tyndale's Bible does not include verses, sections of Scripture were identified by the name of the Bible book, chapter, and a letter. Letters like "K" identified up to several sentences within a paragraph and in this case, the Letter K corresponds with Matthew 22:12.

covert chambers of the print shop. Surely, any shouts of "hallelujah" while in the print shop were kept to a hush to maintain the secrecy.

The Word Gets Out

Despite their precautions, confidentiality was violated. The Roman Catholic scholar named John Dobneck, also known as John Cochlaeus, the dean of a Roman Catholic congregation in Frankfurt,[26] had hired Peter Quentel for a print job. Cochlaeus overheard some of Quentel's staff boasting "confidently in their cups, that, whether the king and cardinal of England would or no, the whole of England would soon be Lutheran."[27]

Intrigued, Cochlaeus later entertained a few of Quentel's workers over a glass of wine, which eventually led to enough liquor to relax their commitment to secrecy. They revealed that two Englishmen had hired their company to print the English New Testaments and that costs were covered by merchants in England. They also mentioned that people would be reading the Bible long before it was discovered on the island nation.[28] Cochlaeus, being an opportunist, quickly approached Herman Rinck, a senator of Cologne and a knight known both to Charles V, the Emperor of the Holy Roman Empire, and King Henry VIII.[29] Rinck, in turn, brought the news to the full senate, which "procured an order interdicting the printers from proceeding further with that work."[30]

Further, Tyndale discovered that his own William Roye had recklessly shared secrets among the printers, jeopardizing their confidentiality and their supporters. Before the further decline of his character,

---

26 Demaus, *William Tyndale*, 112.

27 Mozley, *William Tyndale*, 59.

28 Ibid.

29 Ibid.

30 Demaus, *William Tyndale*, 112.

Roye was a well-known cynical poet who put Cochlaeus's reputation to rhyme:

> *A little, praty, foolish poade,*
> *But although his stature be small,*
> *Yet men say he lacketh no gall,*
> *More venomous than any toad.*[31]

Tyndale's later assessment of Roye holds nothing back, "William Roye, a man somewhat crafty, when he cometh unto new acquaintance, and before he be thorough known, and namely when all is spent, came unto me and offered his help. As long as he had no money, somewhat I could rule him; but as soon as he had gotten him money, he became like himself again."[32] Tyndale, not finished with Roye, talked about how his tongue could "make fools stark mad, but also to deceive the wisest, that is, at the first sight and acquaintance."[33] Here, he makes reference to the instance when Roye deceived his own patron—Humphrey Monmouth, who endorsed him and sent him to the low countries to assist Tyndale.

Upon hearing that Rinck and the Cologne senate was about to arrest them, Tyndale and Roye snatched "away what they could of the finished sheets, and sail[ed] up the Rhine" towards the historic city of Worms.[34]

Meanwhile, Back in England

While Monmouth and his network prayed for and supported Tyndale's ministry in the low countries, no doubt William prayed for Monmouth and other patrons with the fervency that the Apostle John prayed with for Gaius in 3 John 2: "Beloved, I pray that in all respects you may prosper

---

31 Demaus, *William Tyndale*, 113.
32 Tyndale, "Wicked Mammon," in *Doctrinal Treatises*, 37–38.
33 Ibid., 39.
34 Demaus, *William Tyndale*, 108.

and be in good health, just as your soul prospers." In 1525, as Tyndale prepared for the translation of the New Testament, Monmouth faced a time-consuming lawsuit and needed prayer for his business success so that he would continue to be able to support missionaries in a manner most honoring to the Lord.[35] A wealthy man named John Sawyer had included provisions in his will for Monmouth to purchase much of his land before his death. Although Monmouth paid for a significant portion of the land prior to Mr. Sawyer's passing, he had not paid in full by the time Sawyer died on February 4, 1525. Sawyer's daughter, Elizabeth Poole, contested the will and Monmouth's claim to the land. Monmouth's status as the will's executor was perceived as a conflict of interest, so Poole's legal argument seemed to gain strength in her efforts to secure rights to the land.[36] Monmouth was even accused of forging the will. This case dragged through the courts for about ten years, prosecuted by Sir Thomas More, a close friend of Elizabeth's new husband, John Clifford. This created a substantial conflict of interest for More during his prosecution of Humphrey Monmouth from 1528–29. His particular actions and the trial's outcome will be addressed further.

---

35   See Eric Weathers, "Holding the Rope: 3 John for Missions Donors," in *Biblical Missions*, 345–52, for an exposition of 3 John and the necessity for believers to pray for their fellow workers with the truth.

36   Details about Elizabeth Poole-Clifford versus Humphrey Monmouth are available in Andrew Hope's excellent research. See Hope, "Thomas More and Humphrey Monmouth," 244–65.

CHAPTER 6

Smuggling Bibles from Germany to England

And many other signes did Iesus ī the presence of his disciples,
which are not written in this boke. These are written that ye
myght beleve that Iesus is Christ the sonne of God. and that ye in
belevynge myght have life thorewe his name.
John 20:30–31

Background on Reformed Efforts in Germany

Four and a half years before William Tyndale and William Roye arrived in Worms, Germany, Martin Luther was tried for heresy at the Diet of Worms. Giovanni de' Medici, otherwise known as Pope Leo X, along with Charles V, the Emperor, demanded that Luther recant from his teachings or face the death penalty. Luther boldly affirmed his allegiance to the Lord, stating, "My conscience is captive to the Word of God. I cannot and I will not recant anything for to go against conscience is neither right nor safe. God help me. Amen."[1]

A few weeks later, Luther was declared a heretic, his books were banned, and both Charles V and the pope called for his arrest. However, Luther had his own advocates; Frederick the Wise and his guards clandestinely escorted him to Wartburg Castle, where he safely completed his translation of the New Testament into German.

---

1   Andrew S. Ballitch, "Worms, Diet Of," in *The Essential Lexham Dictionary of Church History*, ed. Michael A. G. Haykin (Bellingham, WA: Lexham Press, 2022).

Tyndale's Exile to Worms

By comparison, Tyndale's exile in Worms was relatively safe, as the city's residents valued clear preaching and teaching of God's Word. Nonetheless, confidentiality was crucial. Tyndale's concern about his assistant's loose lips served as a stern reminder to avoid leaking sensitive information.

Peter Schoeffer, Tyndale's printer in Worms, supported William's strategy to print the English Bible as quickly as possible. This decision required the removal of Tyndale's lengthy prologue and glosses, while still allowing space for his brief section encouraging readers to study Scripture in order and context. For Tyndale and Roye, diligence and long hours with the German printers were essential. Given the potential for inaccuracies in typesetting, which would be challenging for the German workers unfamiliar with English technicalities, their oversight was crucial. As a result, the printing process of New Testaments would likely consume their waking hours from late October 1525 through February 1526. Tyndale's warnings about secrecy proved effective; to this day, details of those months remain scarce.

3,000 Printed Bibles, or 6,000?

Since Peter Quentel, Tyndale's printer in Cologne, agreed to only print 3,000 Bibles, there has been confusion as to whether there were 3,000 printed New Testaments shipped to England in the fall of 1526 or 6,000. A close friend of Martin Luther—Georg Spalatin—who served as the secretary to Frederick III, "the elector of Saxony,"[2] who courageously hid Luther in Wartburg Castle in 1521, provides valuable insights into this period. Spalatin documented significant historical details in his journal regarding the 6,000 English New Testaments that were discussed at the Imperial Diet in 1526, held in the town of Speyer,

---

2   Daniell, *William Tyndale*, 67.

near Worms. Spalatin's diary records testimony from Heremann von dem Busche during the Diet, which David Daniell translates: "at Worms six thousand copies of the New Testament have been printed in English."[3]

Further testimony reveals the king's opposition to these Bibles, and his scheme to purchase them, ensuring others could not. Spalatin quotes Busche, stating, "For the English (said Buschius), despite the opposition and unwillingness of the king, so long after the gospel, that they affirm that they will buy the New Testament, even if they must pay 100,000 pieces of money for it."[4] Busche and Spalatin would have been astonished to learn three years later that Cuthbert Tunstall had negotiated a large purchase of Bibles from another of Tyndale's faithful accomplices, Augustine Packington. Packington's clever negotiations with Tunstall will be explored later.

Bibles were cut to size—making them easy to conceal within a coat. Smugglers were prepared to load these Bibles in sacks mixed with commercial goods. That same year, Humphrey Monmouth was elected Warden over the Drapers' Company for the second time.[5] His connections in the wool industry certainly facilitated a role in covert arrangements for Bibles to be hidden among his extensive cloth shipments. As evidenced by Luther's *The Freedom of a Christian Man* and other works, Reformed German merchants were adept at trafficking Reformation literature. These Tyndale supporters had strong ties with textile merchants at the London Steelyard,[6] book buyers in London, and enthusiastic contacts in small hamlets, towns, cities, and universities throughout England.

3   Daniell, *William Tyndale*, 67.

4   Ibid.

5   Fussell to Weathers, May 20, 2025.

6   "Steelyard" is from the Low German word, *Staalhof*, it is way of saying "sample-yard" and has nothing to do with steel. Butterworth and Chester, *George Joye*, 33n1.

Preparing for Export and Import of Contraband

As the frigid winds of the North Sea warmed in the spring, smug-glers in Worms secretly packed New Testaments in cotton bales, flour sacks, barrels of liquid, and bales of cloth on ships bound for England.[7] Even though, as Evan T. Jones points out, "Statutory penalties for smuggling ranged from forfeiture of the goods, to fines, imprisonment and even the death penalty," they pressed on.[8] In 1526, Roman Catholic governance enforced strict adherence to its laws and ordinances; the impression was that only "heretics" with a death wish would be disloyal to the pope and the king. Violating these laws could result in swift and violent judgment.

Meanwhile in England

Tunstall's burning of Lutheran books at St. Paul's Cross in 1521 served to dissuade the possession and distribution of Reformed literature. These types of demonstrations continued until several weeks before Tyndale's Bibles were set to arrive on the shores of England in early to mid-March 1526.

Those committed to receiving the forbidden cargo of Tyndale's Bibles, must have been aware that just about sixteen months earlier, in October 1524, the aggressive "task of vetting all imported books for their heretical views had been assigned not only to Wolsey but also to Warham, Tunstall and Fisher."[9]

This assignment to stamp out Reformed literature precipitated torturous demonstrations January 26 and 27, 1526—just weeks before Tyndale's Bibles were loaded onto ships in Worms. Officials raided the

---

7   Loane, *Masters of the English Reformation*, 72.

8   Jones, *Inside the Illicit Economy*, 43.

9   Peter Gwyn, *The King's Cardinal: The Rise and Fall of Thomas Wolsey* (London: Barrie & Jenkins, 1990), 490.

London Steelyard, searching for Reformation books, which resulted in Dr. Barnes's appearance before the cardinal along with five Steelyard workers who were questioned about their association with Martin Luther's books and "Lollardy."[10] Three weeks later, on February 11, some of Tyndale's associates likely witnessed Cardinal Wolsey preside high above on scaffolding, joined by "thirty-six bishops, abbots and priors."[11] They all heard John Fisher, the Bishop of Rochester, vigorously preaching condemnation on Martin Luther. They would have seen their fellow accomplices, Barns and the five London Steelyard merchants carrying bundles of sticks, twigs and kindling known as "faggots."[12] Mozley says they "marched to a fire which had been kindled, and cast in each his faggot, while great basketfuls of Lutheran books were committed to the flames."[13]

Tyndale's England-based supporters no doubt prayed for their own safety as they prayed for the safe passage of God's Word aboard the ships arriving from Germany. What little sleep was theirs as they begged for the Lord's favor to bring His Word to England and to thwart the king's customs agents from discovering the contraband.[14]

"Segel Setzen!"

With the New Testaments safely stowed, the sailors may have heard the familiar German command, "Segel setzen!" or "Set sail!" This was indeed cause for great rejoicing and eager anticipation for the Lord's

---

10   Foxe, *Acts and Monuments*, 5:417.

11   Mozley, *William Tyndale*, 111.

12   "Like so much else in London, the steelyard was an unapologetic statement of mercantile power and money." Stephen Alford, *London's Triumph: Merchants, Adventurers, and Money in Shakespeare's City* (New York: Bloomsbury, 2017), 1.

13   Mozley, *William Tyndale*, 111.

14   See Jesse Johnson's excellent treatment of how Christians should respond to governmental overreach in *City of Man, Kingdom of God: Why Christians Respect, Obey, and Resist Government* (Pennsauken, NJ: BookBaby, 2022), *passim*.

work in the hearts and minds of those whom the Father gives to the Son (John 6:37).

Flooding England with New Testaments

After the ships docked in England, God ensured safe passage of the Bibles through His Majesty's Customs Services, evading their vigilant eyes "vetting all imported books for their heretical views."[15] The Lord graciously answered the sweet prayers of His people. Once the undetected forbidden books passed by, Tyndale's accomplices transferred the Bibles to booksellers and major universities like Cambridge and Oxford.

Distributors and buyers willing to risk the same fate as Richard Hunne, Dr. Barns, and the five faithful Steelyard men, dispersed Bibles throughout England. Within weeks, commoners, theologians, workers from various livery companies, apprentices, freemen, wardens, the highest level of masters, knights, aldermen, and mayors had their first look at a Bible. People at every socioeconomic and religious level were able to see for themselves that the foundation of their culture deviated from the teachings of the apostles and prophets.

Entire systems were built on lies and deception designed to enslave the masses under a guise of religiosity. For the pope and the king, the greatest threat to national security and their power was Scripture; as Tyndale translated in Hebrews 4:12, it is, "sharper than eny two edge swearde." The people of England were about to read passages like 1 John 1:9, indicating that the unrighteous one has direct access to God who promises to not only forgive sin, but to cleanse the repentant sinner: "yf we knowledge oure synnes, he is faythfull ād iust, to forgeve us oure synnes, ād to clense us frō all unrightewesnes."

When they finally studied the New Testament, starting from the Gospel of Matthew and concluding with the last verse in Revelation, readers were

---

15   Gwyn, *King's Cardinal*, 490.

shocked to find no mention of the "sophistries"[16] taught by the Roman religion, no intimidating bill collectors promising the release of dead relatives from so-called "purgatory," and no need for masses, or Hail Mary's. Instead, they read passages like Galatians 3:11: "That no man is iustified by the lawe in the sight of god is evident. For the iust shall live by faith."

Outrage: The Burnings Begin

The Bibles bore no names on the title page, no indication of the printer's identity, or the city where they were printed. It was too late—6,000 copies were circulating all over the country for about three months before being detected by the "enemyes off the crosse off Christ, whose ende is dampnacion, whose God is their bely and glory to their shame" (Phil 3:18–19).

Already, people had systematically read the translation and were astonished that Jesus' preaching in Matthew 4:17 included the ongoing command to repent. The Lord's commands directly contradicted the teaching they had received for over 1,000 years to "do penance." Matthew's account of Jesus' ministry states, "From thatt tyme Iesus began to preache, ād to saye: repēt, for the kingdōm of hevē is at hōde [hand]" (Matt 4:17).

For those priests and prelates who were untrained in the original languages of the Bible, Tyndale's translation of the Greek word for "repentance"[17] was strange and contrary to their traditional under-

---

16 Tyndale's writings frequently used this word to describe Roman Catholic prelates. About Tyndale's treatise, *Answer to Sir Thomas Moore*, Loane notes that Tyndale "brushed sophistries and subtleties aside to deal with the facts as they were, and his style, plain, terse, vigorous, workmanlike, matched his hard common sense." Loane, *Masters of the English Reformation*, 94.

17 Thomas More did not provide a sound exegetical understanding of the Greek word for "repentance," instead, he resorted to philosophy and tradition. "Sir T. More quotes the preceding words in p. 45 of his Confutation, where he professes to be answering Tyndale's answer to him, and says: 'Here ye see that the sacrament of penance he setteth at less than nought; for he says, It is but a thing forged and contrived to deceive us with. But every good Christian knoweth that such folk as he is, that against the sacrament of penance contrive and forge such false heresies, sore deceive themself, and all them whom the devil blindeth to believe them.'" Tyndale, "Obedience of a Christian Man," in *Doctrinal Treatises*, 260.

standing of "penance,"[18] leading them to label it as heresy. Others rejoiced, recognizing that God's inerrant Word judged the philosophies of men to be the doctrines of false teachers (1 Tim 4:1–3).

Put Down and Burnt

No more than a month after Bishop Fisher's sermon and the humiliation of the Steelyard merchants, Roman Catholic governing authorities were outraged to see New Testaments flooding into their nation. To discourage its widespread effect, the Bishop of London, Cuthbert Tunstall, burned these Bibles, while the enraged Lord Chancelor,[19] Sir Thomas More, burned people.

Susan Brigden's research presents a letter that John Sadler, a London Draper, sent to Richard Harman in Antwerp in September 1526. He issued a warning: "this is the news in England, none other but that the New Testament should be put down and burnt, which God forfend."[20] He boldly declared that the New Testament should be done away with. By "forfend," he meant that God must prohibit the spread of the Bible.[21]

Brigden also discovered that, despite the prohibition and threats, "a City ironmonger, Richard Hall, wrote to Harman in Antwerp, asking for 'two new books of the New Testament in English.'"[22] Richard and his wife, Elizabeth Harman, will later play an important role in Tyndale's ministry in Antwerp. Like so many other committed believers

---

18   Tyndale explained his translation of "repent," in his 1528 treatise, "Obedience of a Christian Man," saying, "of repentance they have made penance, to blind the people, and to make them think that they must take pains, and do some holy deeds, to make satisfaction for their sins; namely such as they enjoin them." Tyndale, "Obedience of a Christian Man," in *Doctrinal Treatises*, 260.

19   King Henry VIII's chief legal counsel.

20   Susan Brigden, *London and the Reformation* (London: Faber & Faber, 1989), 118. Though Butterworth and Chester mentioned this letter in 1962, they did not provide the actual verbiage, see Butterworth and Chester, *George Joye*, 35–36.

21   "Forfend," *Middle English Compendium*, accessed July 31, 2025, https://quod.lib.umich.edu/m/middle-english-dictionary/dictionary?q=forfend&searchfield=anywhere.

22   Brigden, *London and the Reformation*, 118.

in William's life, they provided him with a safe place to reside so that he could produce translations and books to bless the Lord's church for centuries to come.

The Persecution of Accomplices

As the detractors rage grew more furious, and the king's court conspired against the Lord and His anointed, God, who sits in the heavens, laughed and mocked them (Ps 2:2, 4). Tyndale understood this; in 1530, he wrote: "A terrible warning, verily: yea, and look on the stories well, and thou shalt find very few kings, since the beginning of the world, that have not perished from the right way, and that because they would not be learned."[23]

King Henry VIII's commands to keep the English Bible out of his country had no jurisdiction on his Creator. God sovereignly positioned each individual to ensure the delivery of the Bibles in the right place at the right time. The dedication of each supply chain partner was unmatched by Henry, rendering ineffective the threats and abuses from the pope's forces. However, this does not imply that the authorities ceased their efforts to prevent the spread of the gospel; rather, it meant that as the summer of 1526 produced many more Bible readers, the pope's allies took extra measures to implement their counterattack.

In October 1526, Cardinal Wolsey convened the bishops at his palace to formulate a consistent nationwide policy to extinguish the spread of Bibles in England. Among them was Cuthbert Tunstall, whom Tyndale dubbed, "that still Saturn, the imaginer of all mischief."[24] He exemplified Tyndale's impression by persuading other authorities to agree on a plan to confiscate the Bibles. Tunstall instructed them to warn all individuals in their archdeaconries that they must, under threat of

---

23   Tyndale, "Obedience of a Christian Man," in *Doctrinal Treatises*, 242.

24   Ibid., 321.

excommunication and suspicions of heresy, "deliver unto our vicar-general, all and singular such books as contain the translation of the New Testament in the English tongue" within thirty days. Additionally, they must certify the performance of their required actions by letter, "under pain of contempt," within two months.[25]

Some Truth in the Vitriol

Within seven months after the Bibles arrived in England, David Daniell's research indicates that Tunstall was aware that they were the work of William Tyndale and William Roye.[26] On October 25, 1526, Tunstall threatened booksellers, and just two days later, preached a sermon at St. Paul's, publicly denouncing Tyndale and Roye as "maintainers of Luther's sect, blinded through extreme wickedness."[27] While he slandered them for having wandered "from the way of truth," he correctly discerned that they departed from "the Catholic faith."[28]

His accusations continued, and in Foxe's written account of Tunstall's speech, no periods are found, only venomous run-on vitriol declaring that Tyndale craftily "translated the New Testament into our English tongue, intermeddling therewith many heretical articles, and erroneous opinions." Tunstall further charged that Tyndale's New Testament seduced simple people with the use of "perverse interpretations, to profanate the majesty of the Scripture, which hitherto hath remained undefiled."[29]

---

25   Foxe, *Acts and Monuments*, 4:667.

26   Daniell, *William Tyndale*, 175.

27   Francis Aidan Gasquet, *The Eve of the Reformation: Studies in the Religious Life and Thought of the English People in the Period Preceding the Rejection of the Roman Jurisdiction by Henry VIII* (New York: G. P. Putnam's Sons, 1900), 255.

28   Ibid.

29   Foxe, *Acts and Monuments*, 4:667.

The people listening to Tunstall's tirade heard him say that Tyndale craftily abused "the most holy word of God," and that he inserted "many hooks" containing "pestiferous and most pernicious poison." Addressing the reality that the Bibles had spread rapidly in great numbers, Tunstall told his listeners that the Bible "will contaminate and infect the flock committed unto us." He was referring to the prelates sitting high atop the scaffolding, where Cardinal Wolsey presided with "thirty-six bishops, abbots and priors."[30] As Wolsey raised his finger in their direction, Tunstall told his listeners that Tyndale's translation was a "deadly poison and heresy; to the grievous peril and danger of the souls committed to our charge, and the offence of God's divine majesty."[31]

The Impact of Tunstall's Speech

Tunstall's discourse instilled fear in many, including William Tyndale's most heavily invested patron, Humphrey Monmouth, who was in attendance and heard the whole rant. Under the threat of severe consequences, a few years later, Monmouth confessed that until he heard Tunstall's sermon, he had been unaware that Tyndale's New Testament was "noughtilie [naughtily] translated."[32] He admitted: "this was the first time I ever suspected or knew any evil" committed by Tyndale. Monmouth informed Tunstall that he had burned all the books, letters, and treatises Tyndale had sent him. Regarding Tyndale's sermon manuscripts from St. Dunstan's, he stated, "I did burn them in my house." According to his coerced testimony, he did this "for fear of the translator, more than for any ill that [he] knew by them."[33]

---

30 Mozley, *William Tyndale*, 111.

31 Foxe, *Acts and Monuments*, 4:666–67.

32 Strype, *Ecclesiastical Memorials*, vol. 1, pt. 2, 366. A sixteenth century definition of "noughtilie," "had a range of meanings which included abject, evil, wicked, worthless." *Yorkshire Historical Dictionary*, s.v. "noughty," accessed June 3, 2025, https://yorkshiredictionary.york.ac.uk/words/noughty.

33 Strype, *Ecclesiastical Memorials*, vol. 1., pt. 2, 366–67.

More details about Humphrey Monmouth and the nature of his confession will be discussed later. For now, it is sobering to consider that the threats against him were severe enough to compel such drastic actions. The memory of Richard Hunne's murder just eleven years earlier and the persecution of his associates from the London Steelyard, which had occurred weeks before Tunstall's sermon, weighed heavily on his mind. The sacrifices those families endured for their faithfulness were costly. Monmouth's wife (Margery Denham-Monmouth), their daughters (Grace and Elizabeth), his esteemed in-laws (John Denham, the Alderman of London, and his wife, Elizabeth), as well as his multinational business and thousands of employees, all faced potential threats because he contributed to the successful distribution of English Bibles throughout the king's realm.

Tyndale Ally: Francis Denham

History reveals the existence of another Denham, possibly related to Humphrey Monmouth's wife, Margaret, and her parents John and Elizabeth Denham. While we cannot confirm his exact familial ties with Humphrey, it is evident that Francis Denham was a significant ally of William Tyndale. Early in the 1520s, Denham was closely associated with other men who studied law at Inns of Court in London; among them were Simon Fish, James Bainham and Thomas Cromwell, each of whom proved pivotal in William Tyndale's gospel advancing ministry.

God utilized Francis Denham to distribute key Reformation works to influential figures like Thomas Bilney, Simon Fish, and George Constantine.[34] In 1528, while Anne Boleyn was in France, Denham presented her with a French book titled *Pistellis and Gospells for the LII Sondayes in the Yere* [*Epistles and Gospels for 52 Sundays in the Year*].[35]

---

34   Brigden, *London and the Reformation*, 116.

35   Ibid., 116–17.

Anne, of course, later became the second wife of King Henry VIII. In preceding years, a young Francis Denham, likely in his twenties, resided in George Constantine's household in Paris, where he assembled a collection of Luther's tracts and works supporting the French Reformation.[36] Denham admitted that these works included the Greek source material used by Tyndale for his English translation, "novum testamentum Anglice cum introduction ad epistolam Pauli ad Romanos."[37] He was arrested and died from the plague in 1528. It is through believers like Francis Denham that the Lord ensured pastors had biblically sound books in their libraries, enabling them to more effectively communicate God's Word and equip the saints in their churches to do the work of the ministry (Eph 4:12).

Attorney Simon Fish

The Lord also raised up Simon Fish, who was Denham's fellow law student at Inns of Court and another Tyndale advocate. Like Denham, Fish was a prominent provider of Reformation literature. In the year Tyndale's Bibles were smuggled into England, Mr. Fish participated in a Christmas play at Gray's Inn (one of the "Inns of Court" where students studied law), which portrayed Cardinal Wolsey unfavorably. When no one else would take on the role, Simon donned the costume and performed the scene, which offended Wolsey and prompted him to seek revenge. Fearing for his life, Fish "fled over the sea to Tyndale."[38]

Desiring to serve the Lord and to assist Tyndale, Fish translated the Dutch book on biblical doctrine titled *Sum of Scripture*, into English; he also authored *Supplicacyon of Beggers*, a book that attacked various unbiblical Catholic teachings. Research by Susan

---

36 Brigden, *London and the Reformation*, 116–17.
37 Mozley, *William Tyndale*, 349.
38 Foxe, *Acts and Monuments*, 4:657.

Brigden indicates that *Supplicacyon of Beggers* is the same book that Foxe mentions as having been sent to Anne Boleyn, likely in 1528.[39] Anne subsequently presented it to the king, who "kept it in his bosom for three or four days."[40] The king then summoned Mrs. Fish to send for Simon, who, unbeknownst to most people, was actually back in England, secretly hiding less than a mile away. When they met, Foxe recounts, "he came and embraced him with loving countenance."[41] After a few hours of conversing, writing, and hunting together, the king sent Simon home under protection. However, since the king did not provide protection for Mrs. Fish, who possessed a gospel in Latin, the Lord Chancellor had her arrested the next morning; however, due to her daughter's illness with the plague, the chancellor did not trouble her. Within six months, Simon died, and Mrs. Fish married another English Reformer and Tyndale accomplice, James Bainham, the son of a knight in Gloucestershire, not far from where William Tyndale once lived with Sir John and Anne Walsh.[42] James Bainham is a familiar name; like Simon Fish, Bainham was a law student at Inns of Court and a significant partner in William Tyndale's cause, which will be developed in chapter 8.

The selfless bravery of Tyndale and his like-minded partners can encourage believers to carry out their assigned tasks. No single person, including William Tyndale, can accomplish such a mission alone. The body of Christ must work together to fulfill the Great Commission until the end of the age (Matt 28:16–20). Faithful saints must remain vigilant, knowing that He is with them regardless of the depth of the valley or the height of the peaks. We can rejoice in the advancement of the gospel. Amid even our most painful trials, as Romans 8:38–39

---

39   Brigden, *London and the Reformation*, 117.

40   Foxe, *Acts and Monuments*, 4:657.

41   Ibid., 4:658.

42   Ibid.

asserts, "I am sure that nether deeth, nether lyfe, nether angell, nor rule, nether power, nether thynges present, nether thīges to come, nether heyth, nether lowth, nether eny other creature shal be able to departe us from Goddes love, which is in Christ Iesu oure lorde."

Persecution and Prosecution of Tyndale and His Network

These thynges have I sayde unto you because ye shulde
nott be hurte in youre fayth. They shall excomunicat you,
ye the tyme shall come, thatt whosoever killeth you, will thynke
that he doth God true service. And suche thynges will they do
unto you, be cause they have not knowen the father nether yet me.
These thynges have I tolde you, that when that houre is come,
ye shulde remember them, that I tolde you so.
John 16:1–4

Out of love for God and people, Tyndale and his network longed
for their fellow countrymen to know the Lamb of God who can
take their sins away (John 1:29). Nevertheless, in 1528, the 120-year-
old Constitutions of Oxford still remained in effect when several Bible
readers at the University of Oxford were arrested after authorities
discovered 354 prohibited books, including Tyndale's English Bible.[1]

Prisoners entering the Tower of London commonly floated down
the River Thames on a boat toward the Tower; such would be the
case for the arrested students from Oxford who were guilty of reading
Bibles. As they approached the ominous prison fortress through the
Traitors' Gate, they would have been alarmed at the sight of human
skulls belonging to former prisoners dangling overhead, rattling in the
cold wind. However, beheadings were not the cause of their deaths,
since violating the Constitutions of Oxford led to burning at the stake.

---

1   Demaus, *William Tyndale*, 159.

While imprisoned, their studies of the Scripture and of Tyndale's writings prepared them to endure. Tyndale's comments on 2 Timothy 3:12, would have served them well:

> Tribulation for righteousness is not a blessing only, but also a gift that God giveth unto none save his special friends. The apostles rejoiced at being considered worthy to suffer rebuke for Christ's sake. And Paul, in the second epistle and third chapter to Timothy, saith, "All that will live godly in Christ Jesus must suffer persecution."[2]

That year, while many Englanders studied the Word of God and evaded the Roman Catholic governing authorities, William Tyndale's enemies believed he was in Marburg or Wittenberg, producing Bibles with a printer named Hans Luft; he was known for printing Martin Luther's works in Wittenberg and was located over 200 miles east of Marburg.[3] Tyndale cleverly used the city of Marburg and the name "Hans Luft" as decoys to mislead bounty hunters. While they searched for him in Wittenberg, he was actually 400 miles away. Also, when they hunted for him in Hamburg, he was over 300 miles away in Antwerp, a city that offered numerous advantages for Tyndale.

The English House in Antwerp served as a safe haven, akin to modern embassies providing diplomatic protections. Further, a group known as "The Merchant Adventurers," who advocated for English merchants[4] (many of whom, like Richard Harman, were marketplace believers praying for ways to apply their talents and gifts to supply their homeland with sound biblical materials), were based there. These English merchants frequently traveled to and from London. Tyndale's

---

2   William Tyndale, "Obedience of a Christian Man," in *Doctrinal Treatises*, 138.

3   Butterworth and Chester, *George Joye*, 123.

4   Alford, *Merchants, Adventurers, and Money in Shakespeare's City*, 41.

associates, like George Constantine and John Frith, had also sought refuge in Antwerp to escape persecution. Even William Roye, Tyndale's thorn in the flesh, found relief there. Additionally, by 1528, Antwerp boasted around 60 printers, making its printing industry one of the most successful in the region, "producing well over 2,000 titles, or 55% of all books printed in the Low Countries."[5]

At Home with Richard and Elizabeth Harman in Antwerp

As noted in Chapter 6, Richard and Elizabeth Harman played a crucial role in the Lord's hands. The Harmans were arrested in July 1528 for supporting Tyndale's ministry. They were smuggling Bibles into England with their personal resources. It was in their home that Tyndale wrote *The Parable of Wicked Mammon* and *The Obedience of a Christian Man*.[6] The Harmans' contributions were recognized by Anne Boleyn, who would become King Henry VIII's second wife and would personally advocate for their release and reinstatement as English merchants in Antwerp.[7]

Surely, William Tyndale engaged in biblical conversations with the Harmans; his goal for them was the same as for his readers: to grasp biblical doctrines such as justification, forgiveness, the protection of the Holy Spirit, and eternal life. He succinctly expressed this in a 35-word statement: "If thou repent and believe the promises, then God's truth justifieth thee; that is, forgiveth thee thy sins, and sealeth thee with his holy Spirit, and maketh thee heir of everlasting life, through Christ's deservings."[8] Mindful of those who were suffering, he wrote in the same treatise, "Christ is with us until the world's end. Let his little flock

---

5 Alford, *Merchants, Adventurers, and Money in Shakespeare's City*, 43.

6 Hope, "Thomas More and Humphrey Monmouth," 252.

7 Butterworth and Chester, *George Joye*, 128.

8 Tyndale, "Obedience of a Christian Man," in *Doctrinal Treatises*, 262.

be bold therefore. For if God be on our side, what matter maketh it who be against us, be they bishops, cardinals, popes, or whatsoever names they will?"[9] From the Harmans' home, Tyndale taught his readers about sound hermeneutics—the science and art of biblical interpretation. This principle continues to be upheld in pastoral training centers and local churches worldwide: "Thou shalt understand, therefore, that the scripture hath but one sense, which is the literal sense. And that literal sense is the root and ground of all, and the anchor that never faileth."[10] The *Parable of Wicked Mammon* is the first work where Tyndale identified himself as the author; he encouraged the saints to be generous, emphasizing that Christ is Lord over all, including our possessions. It is clear that his generous hosts, the Harmans, were on his mind when he wrote:

> If thy brother or neighbour therefore need, and thou have to help him, and yet shewest not mercy, but withdrawest thy hands from him, then robbest thou him of his own, and art a thief. A Christian man hath Christ's Spirit. Now is Christ a merciful thing: if therefore thou be not merciful after the ensample of Christ, then hast thou not his Spirit.[11]

While these books encouraged the saints, they angered their enemies. Shortly after the printing of *The Parable of Wicked Mammon*, an extensive manhunt was initiated in the low countries. On June 18, 1528, Cardinal Wolsey tasked John Hackett, Henry VIII's agent in the Netherlands, "to get the printers punished, and the authors arrested."[12]

---

9   Tyndale, "Obedience of a Christian Man," in *Doctrinal Treatises*, 135.

10   Ibid., 304.

11   Tyndale, "Wicked Mammon," in *Doctrinal Treatises*, 97.

12   Kingdon, *Incidents in the Lives*, 11.

Wolsey's main targets "appear to have been Tyndale, Roye, and the English merchant Richard Herman [Harman]."[13] As would be the case with Tyndale in 1535, extradition could not proceed without a trial and examination. Hackett's report to Wolsey on July 14 indicated that only Richard Harman was arrested and charged with supporting English heretics and smuggling their books into England, "thus [fomenting] rebellion against the king."[14]

By the time he was in jail for three months, Hackett was unable to provide proof of his charges against Harman. As for Harman, he pressed for a listing of the individuals he was accused of protecting; after several unanswered inquiries to Wolsey, Hackett finally received a report on January 22 that Harman was a patron to "Willem Tandeloo" and "the son of Petit Roy."[15] However, due to insufficient evidence, Harman was released over six months after his arrest.[16]

The financial demands for ministry are great, but the cost believers pay for offending their enemies is even greater. If the Harmans could speak today, quoting Luke 16:9, they would affirm it was worth it: "And I saye also unto you: make you frendes of the wicked mammon, that whē ye shall have nede they may receave you into everlastinge habitacions."

The Manhunts Continue

In September 1528, Herman Rinck, the senator from Cologne who had harassed Tyndale, along with a man named John West from a monastery in Greenwich, embarked on a manhunt for Tyndale and his conspirators in Antwerp, Cologne, and Frankfurt, but to no avail. Their frustration only fueled their aggression, leading to Tyndale being

---

13   Mozley, *William Tyndale*, 129.

14   Ibid., 130.

15   Ibid., 133.

16   Ibid.

labeled a rebellious heretic by January 1529, which intensified efforts to track him down.

Meanwhile, back in England, authorities dispatched their own search parties to identify Tyndale's backers. If they could uncover his patrons and smugglers, they could sever the links in Tyndale's supply chain. Their interrogations revealed a familiar name—they were shocked to learn that Humphrey Monmouth was likely the financial mastermind behind Tyndale's treason against the pope and the king.

The Lingering Impact of Cuthbert Tunstall's Speech on Humphrey Monmouth

When Cuthbert Tunstall threatened booksellers on October 25, 1526, and went on to preach his sermon at St. Paul's two days later, he publicly condemned Tyndale and Roye as "maintainers of Luther's sect, blinded through extreme wickedness."[17] This act of public shaming impacted Monmouth and instilled great fear among the saints in England and beyond.

Nineteen months after Tunstall's threats he made at St. Paul's, on May 14, 1528, Monmouth was summoned to the home of Sir John Dauncies, the father of Thomas More's son-in-law. Present were two prosecutors: Sir Thomas More (who was involved in the Clifford v. Monmouth land case) and Sir William Kingeston (the King's Noble Counsel). Both held significant positions in the Roman Catholic government. According to Monmouth's own handwritten testimony, the men questioned him about any books or letters he had received "from beyond the seas," suspecting he had connections with William Tyndale and hoping to extract useful information through interrogation.[18]

---

17   Foxe, *Acts and Monuments*, 4:666.

18   Strype, *Ecclesiastical Memorials*, vol. 1, pt. 2, 363.

As the examination continued, they inquired whether he had given money to anybody beyond the sea. Monmouth responded, "none and three years past," meaning he had not personally handed money to anyone beyond the sea in the previous three years. They pressed him further, asking if he was acquainted with specific individuals. To the names mentioned, he recalled none but admitted, "three years past I did give unto a priest called Sir William Tyndale, otherwise called Hotchens."[19] When pressed for more details, Humphrey testified that three and a half years earlier, he had heard Tyndale preach at St. Dunstan's in the West and met him after the sermon, curious about "what living he had." Tyndale explained that he had none and that "he trusted to be with my Lord of London in his service," meaning, at that time, Tyndale was awaiting an appointment with Cuthbert Tunstall to gain his permission to translate the Greek Bible into English.[20] Pleased with Tyndale's answer, Monmouth told his inquisitors, "I had the better fantasy [fancy] to him."[21]

Included in his testimony was Tyndale's summary of his meeting with Tunstall, where Tunstall claimed to have "had chaplains enough, and he said to him that he would have no more at any time." Monmouth recalled that Tyndale, homeless and without income, later approached him for assistance, testifying, "the priest came to me again, and besought me to help him, and so I took him into my house half a year: and there he lived like a good priest, as me thought." Monmouth further disclosed that Tyndale studied nearly all day and night, subsisting on minimal food and drink, with unremarkable clothing.[22]

19   Strype, *Ecclesiastical Memorials*, vol. 1, pt. 2, 363.

20   Ibid., 364. For Tyndale's interactions with Tunstall in the hopes of translating the Greek New Testament to English, see chapter 3 above.

21   Strype, *Ecclesiastical Memorials*, vol. 1, pt. 2, 364.

22   Ibid.

As the interrogation progressed, they inquired about the financial support he had provided. Monmouth's response was shrewd, reflecting his knowledge as an experienced businessman. By that time, he had a man named John Marshall serving as his apprentice, highlighting the importance of a "Scripture Man's" role in mentoring or discipling the next generation of godly people in the marketplace.[23] In those days, it was customary to compensate a priest for offering prayers; in this case, Monmouth told the men that he promised Tyndale £10 sterling to pray for his "father and mother there sowles, and al Christen sowles." However, he would not send the money until after Tyndale arrived in Hamburg.[24]

Shrewd Businessman

Humphrey Monmouth did not say, "I gave him money to translate the Bible." Instead, he framed it as the cultural tradition of financially honoring someone for praying. He also noted that Tyndale "got of some other men xl. sterling [£10] more."[25] Just as little is known about most of Paul's fellow workers in Roman 16, not much is known about how many other people supported Tyndale financially. These individuals were Tyndale's allies, providing mission-critical resources to ensure that God's Word would be accessible in what would later become the world's most common language. Monmouth confirmed what is already known about Hans Collenbeeke, the merchant from the Steelyard through whom he funneled the money to Tyndale. With carefully chosen words, he states, "and since I never sent [Tyndale] the value of one peny, nor never will."[26] True, Monmouth may not have ever given Tyndale just

---

23   Fussell to Weathers, May 20, 2025.

24   Strype, *Ecclesiastical Memorials*, vol. 1, pt. 2, 364.

25   Ibid. Small capital and italic original.

26   Ibid.

one single penny all by itself. His gift of £10 had a much higher value: 1,000 pennies.

Monmouth's firsthand account contains a troubling statement: "When I heard my Lord of London [Tunstall] preach at Pawles Cross [Paul's Cross], that Sir William Tyndal had translated the N. Testament in English, and was noughtilie translated, that was the first time that I ever suspected or knew any evil by him." Tunstall's sermon prompted Monmouth to burn all the sermon manuscripts, books, letters, and treatises Tyndale had sent him. But according to his coerced testimony, he acted "for fear of the translator, more than for any yll that [he] knew by them."[27] Though the ashes from Tyndale's sermon manuscripts darkened the air over Monmouth's house, his preaching from God's Word was emblazoned on Monmouth's heart, for "the worde of the lorde endureth ever. And this is the worde which by the gospell was preached amonge you" (1 Pet 1:25). The preaching of God's Word on Sundays fueled Monmouth's passion to serve the Lord every day of the week. After all, it was the Bible which he labored so hard to help mass produce that compelled him to apply it in every element of his life. Afterward, authorities took Monmouth to his house and, in Humphrey's words, "searched it, and saw all the letters and books in my house to my knowledge, by my faith: and there they found no letters that they regarded, nor English books but five or six printed, the which they regarded not; and they left them with me as I found them."[28]

Away to the Tower

After further investigations, the books were finally discovered by the authorities. Eventually, Monmouth was taken to the Tower of London and placed in the custody of "Sir Edmonde Walsyngham, Kt. [Knight]

---

27   Strype, *Ecclesiastical Memorials*, vol. 1, pt. 2, 366–67.

28   Ibid., 364.

And Lyftenant of the Towre," where he remained imprisoned for a year, where he spent much of his time appealing to the authorities to release him, even while William Tyndale continued his ministry in Hamburg, Germany.[29]

An Appeal to Common Generosity

While in the Tower of London, Monmouth testified that supporting ministry students was a regular part of his life. He mentioned giving £40 or £50 sterling to Dr. Royston, one of Tunstall's chaplains, and even much more to Doctor Wooderal and others associated with the king. He challenged his interrogators by asking, "were I to blame for giving them exhibition?"[30] He reminded them that he had given significantly more to many others; he did not do this for praise, but so that the council "should know that [he has] spent more for the love of God, after the counsil of good Doctors, than of that one Priest"— referring to Tyndale.[31] Monmouth's love for supporting students was driven by his love for God; however, his presence in the Tower of London had now destroyed his reputation and "credence, which [he] had, for ever."[32]

An Appeal to the Economy

Monmouth strategically focused on his influence over economic issues. As a man leading a monetary powerhouse as unto Christ (Eph 6:7), the Lord blessed him with significant wealth and placed him in a position to enhance the financial stability of the nation. As far back as 1522, he loaned the king £40, which would be equivalent to approximately $8,096.38 in

---

29   Strype, *Ecclesiastical Memorials*, vol. 1, pt. 2, 364.

30   Ibid., 364–65.

31   Ibid., 365.

32   Ibid., 367.

2025.[33] Cardinal Wolsey, tasked with managing the king's economic affairs, bore the responsibility for the nation's financial performance. If the economy thrived, the king would look good; if it faltered, the blame would rest on Wolsey's shoulders. However, Monmouth's significant role in the textile industry posed a challenge for Wolsey. While imprisoned in the Tower, Monmouth highlighted the plight of cloth workers who struggled to produce clothing without financial resources, leading to unemployment of poor laborers. Notably, the textile industry accounted for one in seven workers.[34] Monmouth lamented that his imprisonment hindered his ability to purchase clothing for manufacturing, which would leave other supply chain members "utterly undon for ever."

Furthermore, the king faced declining duty and tax revenues due to lost sales, being compounded by the financial strain of an escalating war with the Hapsburg Empire. Cardinal Wolsey bore significant responsibility for funding possible military intervention while national security was dependent on his prudent decisions. Before invoking legal reasons for his release, Monmouth expressed: "I trust in the Lord I have not offended your Gr. [Grace] nor none of my lords nor masters of the Kinges noble Counsail, willingly, nor to my knowledg. And yf I have, I beseche your good Gr. and al my lords and masters, to forgive me, as you would that God should forgive you."[35]

An Appeal to the Law

In the year 1515, before having a healthier understanding of the gospel, Monmouth journeyed to Rome where he received a papal pardon.[36]

---

33 Fussell to Weathers, May 20, 2025. As noted in Chapter 4 "Robert Demaus records in his biography of William Tyndale that £10 sterling was "probably a hundred pounds" in his day (1871)", n112, cf. n114.

34 Lee, "Working in the Middle Ages," https://www.medievalists.net/2018/09/working-in-the-middle-ages-the-medieval-clothier/.

35 Strype, *Ecclesiastical Memorials*, vol. 1, pt. 2, 367.

36 Hope, "Thomas More and Humphrey Monmouth," 249.

Little did he know that a trip fourteen years earlier would play such an important role in his being released from the Tower of London. During his deposition, Monmouth contended that if he had broken portions of the Ten Commandments, he had already confessed and been pardoned by the pope during his pilgrimages to both Rome and Jerusalem; thus, he should not be tried further and should be granted forgiveness. He concluded his appeal with respect: "I beseche your Gr. and al my lords and masters, to pardon me of my rude wrytinge and termes. I am unlerned; my witt is no better. By your poor bedman and prysoner at your Gr.'s pleasure, Humfrye Munmouthe, Draper of London."[37]

An Appeal to Grace

It is sobering to reflect on the severity of the actions against Monmouth and the anguish he must have experienced in prison as he recalled the cruelties and threats against those he knew. The memory of Richard Hunne's murder, the persecution of his associates from the London Steelyard, and the sacrifices their families endured for their faithfulness must have afflicted him.

Also to consider, yet again, were the potential threats toward those he cherished most. His family members, international and domestic business partners, and scores of employees up and down the supply chain. Their contributions to the distribution of English Bibles throughout the King's realm marked them for retribution. After numerous appeals for grace and mercy throughout his imprisonment, it is believed that Humphrey Monmouth was released from the Tower of London in the spring of 1529, likely in May.

---

37 Strype, *Ecclesiastical Memorials*, vol. 1, pt. 2, 368.

The Lord's Restoration of Humprey Monmouth

From the time of his release from the Tower through the spring of 1537, Humphrey Monmouth experienced a series of events reminiscent of the drama that played out between Mordecai and Haman in the Book of Esther.

In 1532, the court ruled that the Clifford's accusation of Monmouth forging Elizabeths father's bill of sale was untrue,[38] thus countering Sir Thomas More's influence in the case. In that same year, Humphrey was Warden of the Drapers' Company once again.[39] In 1534, he became Alderman of the Tower, where he had been imprisoned five years earlier. Additionally, due to Sir Thomas More's opposition to the *Act of Supremacy*, which declared the monarch as head of the Church, he resigned as Lord Chancellor of England in 1532. Rather than acknowledge the king's supremacy over the Church, More faced treason charges, punishable by death. On July 6, 1535, Humphrey Monmouth's father-in-law, William Denham, as Sheriff of London, escorted Thomas More to the platform for his beheading; additionally, since Monmouth was the Tower Alderman, he assuredly witnessed More's execution.[40] Two months later, Monmouth assumed the offices of Sherriff and Alderman of London.[41] In 1536, the same year that William Tyndale was martyred, Humphrey Monmouth received the highest honor at the Drapers' Company when he was elected to the position of "Master."[42] In May 1537, it was decreed in court that Monmouth had purchased Elizabeth Clifford's father's land, holding the Cliffords responsible for penalties.[43]

---

38   Hope, "Thomas More and Humphrey Monmouth," 258.

39   Fussell to Weathers, May 20, 2025.

40   Hope, "Thomas More and Humphrey Monmouth," 262.

41   Ibid.

42   Fussell to Weathers, May 20, 2025.

43   Hope, "Thomas More and Humphrey Monmouth," 258.

Monmouth's Final Words

On November 29, 1537, Humphrey Monmouth began his six-page last will and testament with the words: "I, Humphray Monmouth, citezin and alderman of the citie of London, being of whole mynd, and in good and perfect remembraunce, laude and prayse be unto Almyghtye God, make and ordeyne this my present testament."[44] Among the highlights of his will, he commended his soul to Christ Jesus, his Maker and Redeemer, the forgiver of his sins. He appointed men, including Dr. Barns, to preach thirty sermons after his death to the laud and praise of his Lord and Savior, Jesus Christ. He named several individuals, including Thomas Cromwell, to receive specific items from his estate. Monmouth requested that no traditional Catholic ceremonies be held at his funeral. He stipulated that all his debts be settled, that his daughters, Grace and Elizabeth, receive the items he designated for them, and that the child in his wife Margery's womb be included in his wishes. He also left Margery a substantial sum of money and granted her the right to use his house as long as she remained single.

Monmouth demonstrated great love and generosity toward Margery's parents, the Denhams. A review of his will reveals the profound impact of the Word of God on his life; the Lord Jesus Christ was his greatest love. He was a faithful servant of Christ first, a faithful supporter of pastoral students, and a willing accomplice who ensured that the Word of God was accessible to the English-speaking world. For Monmouth, Jesus' Great Commission motivated his service to Christ both at home, in the church, and the marketplace. Humphrey Monmouth went home to be with the Lord, likely on December 13, 1537. Although he may have never read Psalm 116:15, believers like him find joy in the verse: "Precious in the sight of Yahweh is the death of His holy ones."

---

44   Strype, *Ecclesiastical Memorials*, vol. 1, pt. 2, 368.

Tyndale's Hazardous Voyage to Hamburg

As the manhunts continued in 1529, just prior to William Tyndale's perilous journey to Hamburg, Cardinal Wolsey began to pressure the Holy Roman Emperor for action against the production of what he perceived as heretical materials, and Antwerp became less secure for Tyndale and his supporters. Acting on a lead that would provide safe lodging, Tyndale traveled 300 miles northeast to the home of his gracious friend and widow in Germany. He gathered his personal belongings, books, and writing projects which included his recently completed translation of Deuteronomy, intending for it to be printed shortly after his arrival in Hamburg.[45] With everything in order, he set sail.

In mid-March of 1529, as the ship navigated the coast of Holland, a catastrophic shipwreck left William destitute, destroying all his possessions.[46] He lost his books, money, and, most critically, his translations, namely, his print-ready Pentateuch. Yet, God spared his life, for He had greater intentions for Tyndale: "For we knowe wele that all thyngs worke for the best unto thē that love god, which also are called of purpose" (Rom 8:28).

Tyndale Returns to Margaret von Emerson's Home

Upon reaching Hamburg around Easter, 1529, Tyndale, undeterred, began translating the Pentateuch once again. At this point, he had settled in the home of his patron, Margaret von Emerson, the faithful widow.[47] With the assistance of another co-laborer, Myles Coverdale, they continued their work with Margaret's gracious support for the next nine to ten months.

---

45   Foxe, *Acts and Monuments*, 5:120.

46   Ibid.

47   Ibid.

The Von Emerson home served as Tyndale's studio and refuge as the manhunt and assaults against his cause continued. That year, Sir Thomas More had printed *A Dialogue Concerning Heresies* against Tyndale. In October 1529, Charles V, directed by Wolsey, ordered "all copies of the New Testament, in whatever language, to be surrendered for destruction, forbidding any further printing of such books, and condemning heretics to death—the men by the sword, the women by burying alive, the relapsed by fire."[48]

Packington and Tunstall Bible Negotiations

Since Humphrey Monmouth's ordeal, the Roman Catholic governing authorities, under the direction of Cuthbert Tunstall, were fixed on locating Tyndale to the point that Tunstall and Sir Thomas More personally pursued Tyndale in the Low Country. They determined to capture Tyndale by taking it upon themselves to join the manhunt.

Since Tyndale's efforts to avoid capture were so effective, the next best catch for the bounty hunters was to confiscate Bibles he printed. In 1529, while Tunstall and More were in Antwerp searching for what they thought were erroneous translations of the Bible, they encountered Augustine Packington, a man who, Foxe says, "favored Tyndale, but showed the contrary unto the bishop."[49] Packington, with his drive to help Tyndale distribute Bibles, gladly fulfilled their requests for Tyndale's Bibles. While the initiation of this transaction was intended to harm Tyndale, it greatly helped him.

When Tunstall and More engaged Packington and committed to pay handsomely for the New Testaments, Packington saw the opportunity to generate income for his friend. He told his customers that he

---

48   Mozley, *William Tyndale*, 162.

49   Foxe, *Acts and Monuments*, 4:670; John Foxe, *Foxe's Book of Martyrs: A History of the Lives, Sufferings and Triumphant Deaths of the Early Christian and Protestant Martyrs*, ed. William Byron Forbush (New York: Holt, Rinehart, and Winston, 1954), 180.

knew someone who had purchased Bibles from Tyndale in the past and that he probably had more to sell. If Tunstall was willing to guarantee the funds, he would close the deal with the seller who may even be looking to liquidate his entire stock.

Foxe writes, "The bishop, thinking he had God 'by the toe,' said, 'Do your diligence, gentle Master Packington! get them for me, and I will pay whatsoever they cost; for I intend to burn them and destroy them all at Paul's Cross.'"

When Packington relayed this business proposal to Tyndale, William agreed. With a touch of humor, Foxe writes: "The bishop of London had the books, Packington had the thanks, and Tyndale had the money." William Tyndale then utilized the funds to improve his translations and printed numerous updated copies of New Testaments.[50]

---

50   Foxe, *Acts and Monuments*, 4:670.

CHAPTER 8

Faithful to the End

Then I heard a loud voice in heaven, saying,
"Now the salvation, and the power, and the kingdom of
our God and the authority of His Christ have come, for the
accuser of our brothers has been thrown down, he who accuses
them before our God day and night. And they overcame him
because of the blood of the Lamb and because of the word of their
witness, and they did not love their life even to death."[1]
Revelation 12:10–11

A few days before believers celebrated Resurrection Day on April 5, 1529,[2] William Tyndale had been rescued from his shipwreck in the cold waters off the coast of Holland. By Easter, he had found warmth and shelter by the fireplace of Margaret von Emerson, who had been a widow of five years by then. When Margaret's husband, John, had passed away, she was left to care for their six children. Despite facing significant opposition from the senate, two of her sons enrolled at the University of Wittenberg in 1526, the same year Tyndale's New Testaments reached England. Margaret hoped her sons would be educated in biblical doctrine, the original biblical languages, and hermeneutics under esteemed professors like Martin Luther and Philipp Melanchthon. Furthermore, her nephew, Mathias von Emerson, who was Tyndale's classmate in Wittenberg, served the Lord as the Secretary

---

1   *Legacy Standard Bible.*
2   Otherwise known as Easter.

of the London Steelyard where he worked diligently as unto Christ among colleagues until his death.[3]

The relationships between Tyndale, Monmouth, Margaret, and Mathias von Emerson were providentially orchestrated by the Lord to provide William with shelter for two nights in 1524. A year later, Margaret's home likely became a meeting place where Tyndale received funds from Monmouth, delivered by Hans Collenbeeke, the worker from the London Steelyard. It is believed that Hans also brought additional resources from others associated with the Steelyard to Margaret's house. All of these funds were intended to support the Lord's mission to bring His printed Word to the British Isles and the English-speaking world for centuries to come. Thanks to missions-minded friends who were available to the Lord, Tyndale knew that his sister in Christ, Margaret von Emerson, would serve her Savior by assisting him and Coverdale. Despite the ongoing manhunt, Widow von Emerson risked her life by sheltering these two Bible fugitives in her home.

For almost ten months, her residence was a translator's paradise in a world hostile to the truths of the resurrected Savior, whom Margaret loved to serve. During their time together, she encouraged them to persevere. Her warm welcome, exceptional cooking, and unwavering devotion to the Lord made them feel cared for as if they were Jesus Himself (Matt 25:35; 3 John 6).

Her care of the translators must have been remarkable, as evidenced by the prolific works accomplished during their stay. Tyndale, with Coverdale's assistance, translated the Pentateuch and wrote a Prologue. He also began developing other works, including *The Practice of Prelates, A Pathway into the Holy Scripture*, and his *Answer unto Sir Thomas More's Dialogue*.

All seemed well until July 1529, when an illness known as "sweating sickness" struck the townspeople, "where within a month it had swept away no fewer than a thousand persons."[4] While the disease rapidly spread, Tyndale, Coverdale, and Widow von Emerson entrusted their health to the Lord, knowing that nothing was more important than completing their mission. By that time, the harsh winter descended from the arctic, their translations and writings had progressed to a point where relocation was feasible.

The King's Divorce and Other Diversions

Two months before the emperor's edict to kill "heretics" and destroy Bibles in October 1529, King Henry's relentless pursuit of a divorce from Catherine of Aragon intensified.[5] The king had fired Cardinal Wolsey for failing to secure an annulment and had replaced him with Sir Thomas More as Lord Chancellor of England. European universities faced pressure to support Henry's desire to be rid of Catherine, even Parliament in England convened to debate the "Great Matter" and its international political ramifications. The pope refused to grant the divorce. Additionally, Queen Catherine was Emperor Charles V's aunt; thus, the Lord used the distractions of this multinational kerfuffle to reposition Tyndale. He quietly traveled three hundred miles back to the English House in Antwerp to continue his work, while Coverdale accepted a school master position in Germany.[6]

In early 1530, thanks in part to proceeds from negotiations involving Packington and Tunstall, "the first part of his Old Testament translation from the Hebrew began to be taken into England, the five books

---

4   Mozley, *William Tyndale*, 152.

5   Ibid., 162.

6   Ibid., 153.

of the Pentateuch, the only part of the Old testament to be published in his lifetime."[7]

For the first time, English readers studied the Holy Spirit's eyewitness account of creation in Genesis, which William Tyndale translated from within the walls of Widow von Emerson's house:

> In the begynnynge God created heaven and erth, The erth was voyde and emptie, ād darknesse was upon the depe, and the spirite of god moved upon the water. Than God sayd: let there be lyghte and there was lyghte. And God sawe the lyghte that it was good.[8]

Manhunt for Tyndale's Accomplices in England

Humphrey Monmouth's imprisonment from 1528–29 demonstrated the determination of the Roman Catholic governing authorities to find and incarcerate Tyndale's accomplices. Throughout the year 1529, manhunts continued under the direction of the Bishop of London, Cuthbert Tunstall. However, on March 28, 1530, John Stokesley replaced Tunstall as Bishop of London by papal provision and was fully consecrated on November 27 of the same year. Before Tunstall moved from London to Durham, he served a transitional role to allow Stokesley to assume his new responsibilities.[9] Several weeks later, in May of 1530, King Henry enacted a prohibition against Tyndale's

---

7   Buxton, *At the House of Thomas Poyntz*, 26. According to John Foxe, when Sir Thomas More pressed George Constantine to divulge the names of people who supplied funding for Tyndale's Bibles, he said that it was the Bishop of London that gave a great deal of money to burn New Testaments. He testified that Cuthbert Tunstall "is our only succour and comfort." John Foxe, *Acts and Monuments*, 4:671.

8   William Tyndale, *The Pentateuch*, trans. William Tyndale (Marburg, Hesse: Hans Lufft, 1530).

9   Joyce M. Horn, ed., *Fasti Ecclesiae Anglicanae 1300–1541, Volume 5, St Paul's, London* (London: Institute of Historical Research, 1963), 1–4, British History Online, accessed August 21, 2025, https://www.british-history.ac.uk/fasti-ecclesiae/1300-1541/vol5/pp1-4#fnn4.

works, including *The New Testament, The Parable of Wicked Mammon,* and *The Obedience of a Christian Man.* Tunstall, still in transition, quickly acted on Augustine Packington's shrewd negotiations, which provided the Roman Catholic bishop with additional Bibles to burn at Paul's Cross where he directed his second "holocaust of books and Testaments."[10]

Stokesley, too, attacked Christians; in particular, his attacks on William Tyndale's accomplices were marked by severe torture and executions by burning at the stake. A distinction between Tunstall and Stokesley is often made by noting that Tunstall burned Bibles, while Stokesley and More burned people.

Richard Bayfield

John Foxe reported that a young man named Richard Bayfield was saved through the ministry of Dr. Barnes and two godly brickmakers from London—Master Maxwell and Master Stacy—who were influential leaders in their company, rooted in the doctrine of the Lord Jesus Christ.[11] While the Lord equipped Dr. Barnes to lead Bayfield to salvation in Christ, He also prepared brickmakers to transform Richard's life by discipling him with the newly translated English Bible, *The Wicked Mammon,* and *The Obedience of a Christian Man.* One may recall when the Apostle Paul first evangelized the citizens of Thessalonica and how the Lord opened their hearts and minds to the Word. Likewise, the Lord, through Dr. Barnes and two brickmakers, opened Bayfield's ears to the message of the resurrected Christ. Richard received the good news not as mere words crafted by men, but as the inspired Word of God (Acts 17:1–9; 1 Thess 2:13).

---

10   Loane, *Masters of the English Reformation,* 86.

11   Foxe. *Acts and Monuments,* 4:681.

Though Maxwell and Stacy spearheaded their company's success, their careers served as vehicles for bringing the gospel to other nations, as many men and women they led to Christ moved overseas. This prompted Maxwell and Stacy to invest significant amounts of money in order to visit countless disciples and encourage them to faithful service to Christ so that they, in turn, could lead others to repentance. During the next two years, Bayfield's trust in the Lord grew. When his faithful obedience to the Word offended the religious, they threw him into prison. There, he endured nine months of brutality, being gagged, whipped, and locked in stocks. Upon his release, Dr. Barnes took Bayfield to Cambridge for theological training, after which he fled to London, where Maxwell and Stacy secretly took him overseas to meet William Tyndale.

Bayfield excelled in his understanding of Scripture and became a blessing to Tyndale. As a smuggler of Tyndale's books and other German works, he successfully transported them to France and made three significant shipments to England, utilizing different entry points each time. One shipment arrived through the far east, another through Saint Catherine's Dock in central London, where Thomas More confiscated it. However, a load of books and Bibles were successfully smuggled through customs in Norfolk and then transported to London in 1531.[12]

Eventually, Thomas More coerced, presumably under threat of torture, George Constantine to reveal that Bayfield was one of Tyndale's smugglers.[13] By this time, Tunstall had been replaced, and Stokesley and More were aligned with King Henry and the pope, intent on torturing individuals like Bayfield. He was "tied both by the neck, middle, and legs, standing upright by the walls" in an effort to extract the names of other smugglers. Nevertheless, Foxe records that he refused to disclose

---

12   Mozley, *William Tyndale*, 205.

13   Brigden, Susan. *London and the Reformation*, 196.

any names, steadfastly adhering to his faith and convictions until the very end. Richard Bayfield triumphed over his persecutors by the blood of the Lamb and by the word of his testimony; he did not love his life so much as to shrink from death (see Rev 12:11) when he was burned at the stake in November 1531.[14] Nevertheless, in the end, all praise goes to his Savior for a pastor and two brickmakers, along with William Tyndale, for shaping the life of Richard Bayfield.

John Tyndale—The Other Brother

As noted earlier, two of William Tyndale's brothers were Edward, the trade expert, and Thomas, the landowner. The Tyndale family owned considerable property, keeping Thomas occupied with its oversight and business dealings. These brothers likely contributed to William's transla-tion efforts and strategized with others to smuggle Bibles into England.

Additionally, William had a third brother named John, who, unlike him, did not use the surnames "Hutchins" or "Hitchens." John was known for his diligence in the marketplace as a merchant tailor involved in cloth production in the Vale of Berkley, located in Gloucestershire (near the hometown of William Tyndale's family). John's company sourced cloth in the Vale and sold it in London.

Given that the Monmouth families originated from an area located just west of the Tyndales, and that "Edward Tyndale was the most powerful man in the Vale,"[15] it is evident that William, along with his brothers, were well-aware of key figures in the supply chain who could help mastermind the smuggling of Bibles mixed with textile cargoes bound for England.[16]

---

14   Daniell, *William Tyndale*, 184.

15   Ibid., 15.

16   Ibid.

On February 28, 1528, John Tyndale encountered a clothmaker named Boswell who asked him to purchase his goods, but John declined the offer. Like any seasoned solutions oriented salesperson, Boswell, seeking to overcome John's objections, asked for the reasoning behind his decision. John straightforwardly replied that he could not find buyers to cover his costs. Pressing further, John told Boswell that commoners must unite their voices and complain to the king about how economic conditions have forced people to unemployment.[17] Two months later, this financial hardship worsened when a significant contributor to the textile industry, Humphrey Monmouth, was imprisoned in the Tower of London over suspicions of aiding William Tyndale.

As a prudent steward, John Tyndale recognized that closing the unprofitable deal with Boswell would jeopardize his financial support for William's translation ministry. Also, he later testified to having donated money, a total of five marks, to William, which was approximately four to five months' income for a highly skilled laborer.[18] More than just a major donor, John actively distributed William's Bibles and books. Shortly after William printed his 1530 translation in Antwerp, he covertly sent some New Testaments to John and his conspirator, Thomas Patmore, a young London merchant. Together, they dispersed the books to readers throughout England.[19] Details describing how the activities of these men were discovered are sparse, but they were eventually arrested and faced the wrath of John Stokesley.

Exercising his new authority, Stokesley arrested John Tyndale and Thomas Patmore, bringing them to Sir Thomas More, who took them to Star Chamber for judgment and sentencing. Star Chamber is where high-ranking royal officials adjudicated prominent cases and tended to

---

17   Mozley, *William Tyndale*, 121–22.

18   Foxe, *Acts and Monuments*, 5:29.

19   John Strype, *Memorials of the Most Reverend Father in God Thomas Cranmer, Sometime Lord Archbishop of Canterbury*, vol. 1 (London: Richard Chiswell, 1694), 116.

important government business. Tyndale's and Patmore's punishment was to "ride with their faces to the horse tail, having papers on their heads, and the New Testaments and other books (which they dispersed) to be fastened thick about them, pinned or tacked to their gowns or cloaks."[20] With their faces uncomfortably close to the horses' posteriors, they were subjected to animal excrement, with only paper protecting their heads. Upon arrival at their destination, they were forced to throw the papers, books, and Bibles into the flames and pay the king's fine.[21]

Though John Tyndale had been excommunicated and abjured for his crimes, he was known for pretending his penance and giving insincere denials of his faith in order to continue evangelizing. Essentially, John acted like a parrot, repeating whatever words his captors demanded, allowing him to remain active in ministry through the 1540s.[22] In the end, God used the partnership of these two brothers to advance the gospel: one a faithful scholar who translated the Bible from Greek and Hebrew to English, the other a faithful businessman who donated financial resources and supply chain expertise to ensure that God's Word reached the English-speaking people for hundreds of years.

James and Mrs. Bainham

James Bainham was a law student in the early 1520s who was closely associated with other men at the Inns of Court, including Francis Denham, who is believed to be a relative of Humphrey Monmouth through his wife, Margery Denham-Monmouth.

Reputed for his godliness and dedication to studying law at the Inns of Court, his character reflected the qualities of elders, as described in 1 Timothy 3 and Titus 1. Foxe characterized James as having a "virtuous

---

20   Strype, *Memorials of Thomas Cranmer*, 116.

21   Ibid.

22   Brigden, *London and the Reformation*, 191.

disposition," engaging in "godly conversations," being "mightily addicted to prayer," and being well-known as "an earnest reader of Scriptures." His character was described as irreproachable. He was known as "a great maintainer of the godly" and "a visitor of the prisoners." Bainham was kind to fellow scholars and "merciful to his clients," ensuring that justice was equitably administered to the poor. He counseled the needy, particularly the widows, orphans, and the financially distressed. Foxe summarized Bainham's reputation succinctly: "briefly, a singular example to all lawyers."[23] James Bainham's mental and moral qualities serve as a model for all saints, especially those in legal professions.

James married the widow of his close friend, Simon Fish, the fellow law student who mocked Cardinal Wolsey, which led to his exile to the low countries to join Tyndale. The work he completed there, *Supplicacyon of Beggers,* so impressed King Henry VIII that Fish was granted personal protections. However, those protections did not extend to his wife, who was arrested for possessing copies of the gospel and briefly incarcerated. Her husband Simon passed away six months later. Shortly after, she became Mrs. James Bainham.

Although historical evidence has not confirmed that James Bainham ever met William Tyndale, he is regarded as one of Tyndale's accomplices. Bainham's elder qualities (see 1 Tim 3:2–7) encouraged his fellow saints, but they enraged the enemies of the cross who labeled him as a heretic.

It did not take long for the Lord Chancellor, Sir Thomas More, a graduate from Lincoln's Inn—one of four Inns of Court—to bring up Bainham on charges of "heresy." More arrested him and had him taken into custody by the sergeant-at-arms, who escorted him from the Middle Temple, another prestigious Inn of Court known for training lawyers. Bainham was brought to More's house, where the Lord Chancellor attempted to intimidate him into renouncing his trust in the Word of God. Every effort failed, leading More to confine him to his

---

23   Foxe, *Acts and Monuments,* 4:697.

household prison. According to Bainham, More accused him of affirming that it is legal for all men and women to own a Bible in their own language, that the pope is the Antichrist, that there are no other keys to heaven's gate except the preaching of the law and the gospel. Further, that there is no purgatory but the purgatory of Christ's blood, and that at the moment of death, believers' souls immediately enter heaven and are at rest with Jesus forever.[24]

Bound to More's Tree of Truth

To extract information and secure Roman Catholic penance, More bound Bainham to his "Tree of Truth," or as Foxe writes, the "Tree of Troth,"[25] and brutally whipped him in his exquisitely manicured garden. When this failed to achieve More's objectives, he placed Bainham on a boat that sailed down the River Thames. The skulls of former prisoners dangling from the overhead bridge greeted him at the Traitor's Gate at the entrance to the Tower of London. Bainham, by this time, would have studied passages in Tyndale's translation of the New Testament and understood that fellow saints would suffer for their association with the crucified Christ. Would he have been sustained by the verses Tyndale recently translated? Perhaps. Paul says in in Philippians 1:19–21:

> For I knowe that this shalbe for my health, thorowe youre prayer, ād ministrīge of the sprete of Iesu Christ, as I hertely loke fore ād hope, that ī nothīge I shalbe ashamed: but that with all confidence, as allwayes in tymes past, even soo nowe Christ shalbe magnified in my body, whether it be thorowe lyfe, or els deeth. For Christ is to me lyfe, and deeth is to me avauntage.

24   Foxe, *Acts and Monuments*, 4:705.

25   Ibid., 4:698.

Taken directly from the boat, he was placed on a hard wooden rack where prison officials stretched Bainham's limbs in opposite directions, causing his joints to separate and forcing him to gasp for air. During this ordeal, Sir Thomas More pressured him to reveal the location of his books and to name his fellow believers in the Middle Temple. When James refused to disclose the whereabouts of his library, Thomas More attempted to intimidate Mrs. Bainham into disclosing them. After her refusal, she was sent to the Prison Fleet, and their worldly belongings were confiscated.[26]

Ready in Season and Out of Season

On December 15, 1531, More continued his relentless interrogation of Bainham. Foxe records nine questions posed to him, detailing his responses to each. His answers revealed not only that he was a well-educated attorney but also that he was a knowledgeable Bible scholar. It did not matter to him that he was facing death, he was in season, ready to "reprove, rebuke, exhort, with great patience and instruction" (2 Tim 4:2). When asked about his belief in purgatory, Bainham cited Scripture, quoting William Tyndale's recent translation. With the authority of 1 John 1:7–9, Bainham boldly evangelized More, saying:

> If we walk in light, even as he is in light, we have society together with him, and the blood of Jesus Christ his Son hath cleansed us from all sin. If we say we have no sin, we deceive ourselves, and the truth is not in us. If we confess our sins, he is faithful and just, and will forgive us our sins, and will purge us from all our iniquities.[27]

---

26   Foxe, *Acts and Monuments*, 4:698.

27   Ibid.

Roman Catholic tradition, lacking biblical authority, claims that "purgatory" is a place where departed souls may be "purged," being contingent upon the amount of monetary contributions made by surviving relatives to the pope's bill collector in order to "purge" them from purgatory. In contrast, Bainham's answers were rooted in the authoritative Word of God, which teaches that God alone "purges" the repentant from their iniquities. Thomas More presented Bainham with multiple opportunities to "return to the catholic church, from whence he was fallen and to which he might be received; the bosom of his mother was open for him."[28]

Several weeks later, in February 1532, Bainham was again confronted with the articles of his alleged crimes, given one last opportunity to recant. Foxe notes that Bainham ultimately yielded to their threats and returned to the Catholic faith. To complete the process, Bainham was required to read a statement: "I voluntarily, as a true penitent person returned from my heresies, utterly abjure," however, partway through, he stopped because he believed the responses he had given during his interrogation were not heretical. Thomas More then continued reading from where Bainham had paused, adding the words "the doctrine and determination of the church;"[29] then he stopped, waiting for Bainham to comply. He did not.

Bainham was returned to prison for five days. On February 8, 1532, he was given another opportunity to recant; this time, he agreed to abandon his previous answers, agreeing to "meddle no more with them."[30] He read the required words aloud, paid a twenty-pound fine to the king, carried a faggot to Paul's Cross, and was finally released to go home. Overwhelmed with grief and regret, less than a month later, Bainham entered St. Austin's Church with his New Testament and

---

28   Foxe, *Acts and Monuments*, 4:700.

29   Ibid., 4:701.

30   Ibid.

The Obedience of a Christian Man. He stood to his feet and confessed, "weeping in tears, that he had denied God,"[31] pleading for the people's forgiveness and urging them not to follow his example. Shortly after, he was arrested again and subjected to the flames.

Courage at the Stake

In May 1532, James Bainham stood at the stake, viewing it not as an instrument of death, but as an opportunity to evangelize the lost, to confront the sinful pope, and to encourage those saved by God's grace. As the chain tightened around his chest, just before the flames were ignited, he said that Thomas More's accusations, for which he must die, "be very truth, and grounded on God's word, and no heresy."[32] While chained to the wooden pole, he proclaimed to the crowd that it is lawful for everyone to have God's Word in their own language, warning them that the pope is the Antichrist. He declared that the only key to heaven is the preaching of God's Word. As the chain constricted further, he declared that there is no purgatory, stating that only Christ's blood purges sins, and that the souls of the redeemed go to heaven for eternal rest with Jesus Christ. Additional accusations were hurled against him, followed by his sobering words of truth. According to Foxe, "as the train of gunpowder came toward him, he lifted up his eyes and hands unto heaven, and said to Pave, his executioner: 'God forgive thee, and show thee more mercy than thou showest to me: the Lord forgive sir Thomas More! And pray for me, all good people.'"[33]

---

31   Foxe, *Acts and Monuments*, 4:702.

32   Ibid., 4:705.

33   Ibid., 4:704.

John Frith

One of the Oxford University students arrested for reading the Bible was released by the king on condition that he stay within ten miles of Oxford.[34] However, John Frith, following the deaths of his fellow students in 1528, fled overseas to Antwerp.

The scholar was known for his strong arguments against Catholic teachings on purgatory and for providing compelling biblical instructions for the Lord's Supper that contradicted Roman Catholic doctrines. In 1532, Frith was rearrested and sent back to the Tower of London, where he led Sir Thomas More's brother-in-law to the Lord.[35] Tyndale nicknamed Thomas More "The Proctor of Purgatory"[36] because he ardently defended Catholic teachings on the topic. More argued against Martin Luther and William Tyndale's doctrinal positions in which they found no biblical basis for purgatory. More also wrote a treatise known as *Supplication of Souls*, which was his response to Simon Fish's *Supplication of Beggars*, which also took issue with the unbiblical teachings of purgatory.

Young Frith endured captivity in the cold and miserable confines of the tower, where chilling winds blew through its arrow slits, the narrow, cross-shaped openings in the walls where archers launched their arrows. Could these crosses, which also let in the light, serve to remind the captives of the crucified yet resurrected Lord (1 Cor 15:12–49)?

A Godly Wife's Encouragement

In May 1533, about two months before Frith's execution, William Tyndale sent him a letter from Antwerp to embolden his brother in Christ. The letter included an encouraging message from Frith's godly

---

34   Mozley, *William Tyndale*, 121.

35   Ibid., 254.

36   Tyndale, *The Practice of Prelates*, in *Expositions and Notes*, 335.

wife, which released him from concern about her well-being so as not to detract from God's glory. It stated, "Sir, your wife is well content with the will of God, and would not, for her sake, have the glory of God hindered."[37]

Tyndale comforted Frith by reminding him that he was not suffering alone, mentioning others who had faithfully endured before him:

> Two have suffered in Antwerp, unto the great glory of the gospel; four at Risele in Flanders, and at Lucca hath there one at the least suffered; and all the same day. At Rouen in France they persecute, and at Paris are five doctors taken for the gospel. See, you are not alone; be cheerful, and remember that among the hard hearted in England, there is a number reserved by grace; for whose sakes, if need be, you must be ready to suffer.[38]

John Frith was burned at the stake in Smithfield on July 4, 1533. As for his enemy, Frith:

> *overcame him because of the blood of the Lamb*
> *and because of the word of [his] witness,*
> *and [he] did not love [his] life*
> *even to death*
> Revelation 12:11

---

37   Foxe, *Acts and Monuments*, 5:132.

38   Ibid.

CHAPTER 9

Though Dead, He Still Lives

Verely I saye unto you, there ys no man that hath forsaken housse,
or brethren, or sisters, or father, or moder, or wyfe, other chyldren,
or londes, for my sake and the gospelles, whych shall nott receave
an houndred foolde nowe in thys lyfe, housses, and brethrē, and
sisters, and mothers and childrē, and londes whith persecucions,
and in the worlde to come eternall lyfe.
Mark 10:29–30

illiam Tyndale and his Great Commission–minded brothers and sisters in Christ risked everything to produce and deliver the Scriptures in the English language. The laws of the land and the prevailing animosity against them meant that they would be loathed, hunted, and persecuted to the point of death. Though they forsook homes and family for Jesus' name and the sake of the gospel, they received so much more, including multitudes of brothers and sisters in Christ for eternity.

Because God used faithful people to accomplish His purposes, English readers, for the first time, studied God's plan of salvation for themselves. Those who read the New Testament from 1526 through 1534 and beyond were astonished by the absence of concepts such as purgatory, interceding for the dead, or praying to Mary and the saints. They found no instructions for Christians to worship relics, and they were met with a deafening silence about doing penance and taking pilgrimages to Rome. Their government was based on a religious system established by biblically unqualified leaders (1 Tim 3:1–7; Titus 1:5–9; 1 Pet 3:1–3) who claimed that their pope descended from the Apostle Peter through apostolic succession. For these reasons and many more, the Bible was attacked because the Word of God threatened to dismantle their religion and culture.

By the time we locate William Tyndale in Antwerp in 1534, it is evident that the Lord had protected him from the penalties of the 1408 Constitutions of Oxford since his arrival in Little Sodbury in 1522. Every attempt to halt the proliferation of God's Word was unsuccessful. The King of England, the Emperor of the Holy Roman Empire, the pope, and every bishop, cardinal, lawyer, and bounty hunter were dismayed that their well-orchestrated strategies resulted in failure. Threats of death did not deter him; Bible bonfires inflamed the passion for God's Word in the hearts of men and women. No slander, rack, whip, public humiliation, nor even burning at the stake could prevent him from ensuring that the plowboy would know God's Word better than the pope. God's love for men, women, children, and subsequent generations endured for more than 500 years as His people declared His glory among the nations (cf. Ps 96).

The Apostle Paul chose Phoebe—the first-century courier of the sixteenth-century Reformation—to deliver his letter to the Roman churches nearly 1,500 years earlier. This letter ultimately made it to the hands of William Tyndale and was included with 26 other New Testament books that impacted the hearts and minds of the English church in 1526. Neither Tyndale nor his "fellow workers with the truth" (3 John 8) were the main focus—very few people knew of them in 1526. However, as John Foxe notes, William Tyndale "is justly styled The worthy Apostle of the English Reformation;"[1] additionally, now on the 500th anniversary of his 1526 translation, he stands as an ambassador to more than one and a half billion English speakers around the globe,[2] but further attention given to those who risked their lives with him is essential.

---

1   Foxe, *Acts and Monuments*, 5:114n3.

2   Adam Zeidan, "Languages by Total Number of Speakers," in *Encyclopædia Britannica*, accessed July 31, 2025, https://www.britannica.com/topic/languages-by-total-number-of-speakers-2228881.

Thomas and Anna Poyntz

In 1534, the Lord brought William Tyndale into the home of Thomas and Anna Poyntz, proprietors of the English House in Antwerp. The English House was the safest place for Tyndale to continue his translations and writing. Here, God used Thomas and Anna to provide an environment where Tyndale could integrate with other English merchants while remaining relatively protected from local criminals and governing authorities who exploited foreigners.

Thomas Poyntz was a member of the renowned Poyntz family, which had established connections with the Tudor royal court since the 1470s.[3] His childhood home was in North Ockendon, Essex, 130 miles from his relative, Robert Poyntz of Iron Acton. Robert Poyntz' son, Sir Anthony Poyntz, served as Sheriff of Gloucester and commanded a fleet of forty-two ships bound for France.[4] King Henry VIII favored him, and he eventually became the King's Steward over significant portions of Gloucestershire.[5] In 1535, shortly before William Tyndale was arrested in Antwerp, King Henry and Queen Anne Boleyn spent two nights in the home of Sir Anthony's son, Nicholas, who appeared sympathetic to the Reformation.[6] The connections between Thomas Poyntz and King Henry VIII are significant, as they demonstrate Poyntz's efforts to leverage these relationships to persuade the king to intercede with Charles V for Tyndale's release from prison.

---

3   Daniell, *William Tyndale*, 55.

4   John Maclean, *Historical and Genealogical Memoir of the Family of Poyntz*, pt. 1 (Exeter: William Pollard, 1886), 67.

5   Hoyle, *Military Survey of Gloucestershire, passim.*

6   Daniell, *William Tyndale*, 35.

Connections with Queen Catherine of Aragon and a Famous Grandfather

It is also worth noting that Thomas Poyntz's brother John was associated with "Queen Katherine of Arragon as one of the Sewers of the Queen's Chamber."[7] John "was in attendance upon her at the magnificent interview between the Kings of England and France, commonly known as the 'Field of the Cloth of Gold,' in 1520."[8] Additionally, Thomas was connected to royalty through his maternal grandfather, Edmond Shaa, who served as Mayor of London and the King's official goldsmith.[9] Under Shaa's guidance, Thomas's father, William, was appointed as the engraver of the tower mint. Subsequently, Thomas's brother John became the master of the mint, a member of parliament, and prime warden for the Goldsmiths' Company, eventually rising to the positions of Alderman, Sheriff, and Mayor of London.[10]

Family Connections and Business Dealings

By the Lord's providence, the Tyndale, Walsh, Poyntz, and Monmouth families were connected through shared business dealings that trace back to Gloucestershire and the textile industry. By 1517, Thomas Poyntz was a freeman in the Grocers' Company, trading in spices and pharmaceuticals. His home was strategically situated near one of his largest customers, a hospital dedicated to Thomas Becket in the thirteenth century, close to St. Paul's Cathedral. As a Merchant Adventurer,[11] Poyntz's diverse business interests included the wool trade, positioning him well as an importer and exporter. His expertise and professional

7   MacLean, *Memoir of the Family of Poyntz*, 33.

8   Ibid.

9   Kingdon, *Incidents in the Lives*, 7.

10   Buxton, *At the House of Thomas Poyntz*, 11.

11   Kingdon, *Incidents in the Lives*, 9.

network facilitated his move to Antwerp in around 1526, where the Lord provided him with a bride from the local area—Anna van Calva. Together, they had four children and played a crucial role in managing the English House.

Until July 1534, Humphrey Monmouth was believed to have been the governor of the English House, where Thomas and Anna Poyntz hosted merchants, and also William Tyndale.[12] It was there in Antwerp that Tyndale had the opportunity to work on revising his translation of the New Testament, along with writing a nine-page greeting for his updated 1534 edition of the New Testament, which opens with these words: "W. T. UNTO THE READER / Here thou hast (most dear reader) the new testament or covenant made with us of God in Christ's blood."[13] Tyndale diligently compared his translation with the Greek text, claiming to have "weeded out of it many faults." He encouraged his critics to examine the original grammar to substantiate their critiques, aiming to refine the translation for English readers. He emphasized the difference between biblical repentance and Roman Catholic doing of "penance." He clarified the term "elder" in contrast to "priest," and provided a synopsis of each of the four Gospels, concluding with a warning from Matthew 23:26.

Connections through the English House

The frequent arrivals and departures of the English House meant that Tyndale mingled with many English merchants. Foxe notes that he was known to go "forth to dinner and supper among merchants,"[14] suggesting he ventured outside the English House to build and strengthen relationships, some of them which likely facilitated the smuggling of

---

12   Buxton, *At the House of Thomas Poyntz*, 28.

13   William Tyndale, *Tyndale's New Testament: A Modern-Spelling Edition of the 1534 Translation*, ed. David Daniell (New Haven, CT: Yale University Press, 1995), 3.

14   Foxe, *Acts and Monuments*, 5:122.

his 1534 edition to England and beyond. While Tyndale remained vigilant, he was also concerned for the souls around him. Given his passion for preaching and teaching, he would have encouraged many merchants and Christian refugees with Bible studies and Sunday gatherings for like-minded believers and those the Lord was drawing to Himself. Although the English House was the safest place for his ministry, the rights and privileges of its residents applied only within its walls. Once outside, Tyndale faced the same dangers as any other English merchant; however, as a long sought after fugitive from England with a bounty on his head, harbored by his lesser-known accomplices, he was exposed even further than the rest.

Strained Relations in the Low Country

Additionally, a series of events related to the King's divorce from his first wife caused the Low Country to become a more dangerous location for Tyndale than England. In 1533, England enacted the Act in Restraint of Appeals, which removed papal authority over the English church. The following year, the Act of Supremacy declared the English Monarch as the head of the English church,[15] disregarding the characteristics of an elder in 1 Timothy 3, Titus 1, and 1 Peter 3:1–3. With these new laws, the pope's refusal to grant Henry's divorce from Catherine became irrelevant, placing the king in conflict with Charles V, Catherine's nephew and a subordinate to the pope.

Relations between England and the low countries became strained, making favors between Henry and Charles unwelcome. Such tensions became the reason why Tyndale might have been slightly safer in England than in Antwerp, where his crime was less about translating the Bible into English and more about violating Roman Catholic tradition. England's Act in Restraint of Appeals meant that the pope's

---

15   Inwood, *A History of London*, 151.

control over protestant religious practices was not the same as his power over Charles V's dominion in the low countries. Henry's new power served to strengthen Charles's resolve to punish violators of Roman Catholic dogma. Nevertheless, while Tyndale remained in Antwerp, he was subject to the laws of the Holy Roman Empire and its emperor, Charles V.

It is uncertain whether Poyntz or Tyndale were aware of a new cry in England as evidenced by people reading and hearing the Word of God, confessing that Jesus is Lord, and believing in their hearts that God raised Him from the dead, resulting in their salvation, just as "the scripture sayth: whosoever beleveth on hym, shall not be ashamed" (Rom 10:11). "On December 19, 1534, the upper house of the convocation of Canterbury passed a resolution, begging the king to have a new translation made."[16] Although their pleas seemed to go unheard, the Lord was at work, building His church and overcoming every stronghold. Nearly a year later, while Tyndale and Poyntz faced severe repercussions, the Coverdale Bible (containing both the Old and New Testaments), was printed in October 1535, likely in Antwerp.

It was not until 1537 that King Henry VIII finally allowed a Bible to be published in England. That Bible was produced by John Rogers under the assumed name of "Thomas Matthew," who was also associated with William Tyndale. Rogers incorporated much of Tyndale's Old Testament translations, combining them with Coverdale's work to unite a complete Bible, known both as the "Matthew Bible" and "The Great Bible," which also earned King Henry VIII's approval.[17] The Matthew Bible was finally printed and distributed in 1538 to churches in England. The Great Bible earned its name because of its massive size and extremely high cost of production. Because it was so expensive,

---

16 Mozley, *William Tyndale*, 266.

17 Walter A. Elwell and Philip Wesley Comfort, *Tyndale Bible Dictionary*, Tyndale Reference Library (Wheaton, IL: Tyndale House Publishers, 2001), 205.

the Great Bible was also known as the "Chained Bible." It was called "Chained" because it was fastened to church pulpits to keep people from stealing it.

Henry Phillips: A New Friend or a Fatal Foe?

Although the king freed England from papal control, the 1408 Constitutions of Oxford still governed the land, keeping Tyndale and his associates as targets of prosecution. Despite numerous attempts to capture him, his enemies continued plotting his downfall to no avail, until a man named Henry Phillips accepted the challenge.

As the son of a three-time Member of Parliament and a former sheriff, Henry Phillips had the honor of receiving invitations to Queen Anne's wedding celebrations in 1533.[18] Foxe described him as an attractive young gentleman accompanied by a servant, indicating he was affluent and well educated.[19] Records show that he earned a Bachelor of Civil Law from Oxford in 1533 and was fluent in Latin.[20] After graduation, Phillips violated his father's trust by failing to deliver a large sum of money to a business associate in London. Lured by temptation, he squandered his father's money on gambling and was too ashamed to return home, "for the next several years he approached his patrons for rescue, to no avail."[21] Impoverished and unwilling to confess his crime, he likely accepted a bribe from a London official to find Tyndale and bring him to justice, hoping that his success would earn him a reward and allow him to repay his father.

Phillips journeyed to Louvain in the low countries, near Antwerp, where he was welcomed as a student at a papal stronghold with a

18   Daniell, *William Tyndale*, 361–62.

19   Foxe, *Acts and Monuments*, 5:121–22.

20   Buxton, *At the House of Thomas Poyntz*, 31.

21   Daniell, *William Tyndale*, 362.

university.[22] Since Tyndale rejected the doctrines taught at Louvain, Phillips found support from loyalists to finance his efforts to locate and arrest Tyndale for being an adversary of their Roman Catholic causes.[23] After discovering that William Tyndale was living under the protection of the English House, Phillips realized he needed to befriend not only Tyndale but also those close to him. Eventually, he learned that Tyndale was staying with Thomas and Anna Poyntz. He quickly ingratiated himself with Tyndale during meetings with him in the homes of other merchants. After several interactions and meals, he finally shared many mealtimes in the Poyntz home. Phillips's demeanor, theological understanding, and educational background led Tyndale to trust him. Thomas Poyntz, however, did not trust Phillips and warned Tyndale to be cautious. Undeterred, Phillips deceived the translator into believing he was a reliable friend. When Thomas left for business matters for several days, Phillips visited Anna Poyntz, inquiring if he could have dinner with Tyndale. He then informed the arresting officers to position themselves behind a door on a narrow street so that they could capture Tyndale as he accompanied him to dinner.

A Judas-Styled Betrayal

Phillips returned to the Poyntz house, where Tyndale was ready to head out. Phillips offered to pay for their meal but claimed he had forgotten his money and asked Tyndale for a loan of forty shillings, which Tyndale readily provided to his new friend. As they walked down the narrow passageway, Phillips kindly gestured for Tyndale to go ahead. At that moment, officers lurking behind the door saw Phillips pointing over Tyndale's head and seized him. On May 21, 1535, after an eleven-year

22　Mozley, *William Tyndale*, 298–99.
23　Foxe, *Acts and Monuments*, 5:128.

exile, Tyndale was finally arrested;[24] he was taken to Vilvoorde Castle, six miles from both Brussels and Louvain.[25] Shortly after arriving at the prison, he was taken to dinner by the emperor's attorney; afterward, the Procurator-General Pierre Dufief came to Poyntz's home to confiscate Tyndale's belongings, including his books.[26] Dufief's visit was likely the first indication to Anna Poyntz that Tyndale had been arrested. The primary reason for Tyndale's capture was violation of local religious ordinances established by the University of Louvain, which were ultimately directed by the pope and enforced by local law enforcement.

Thomas Poyntz's Rescue Mission for William Tyndale

It is unclear whether Anna Poyntz dispatched messages to her husband about Tyndale's arrest or if she waited for him to return to Antwerp. Regardless, it seems that many days passed before Thomas finally learned of William's detention at Vilvoorde Castle.[27] Evidence suggests that merchants at the English House were immediately aware of their fellow Englishman's arrest. They undoubtedly witnessed Pierre Dufief enter their refuge and seize a fellow merchant's belongings. In response, they quickly sent letters to the court in Brussels, expressing deep concern over this violation of their trust and the mistreatment of a fellow merchant under diplomatic protection.[28] They wanted Brussels to understand that such actions could jeopardize international trade.

In an effort to save William Tyndale's life, Thomas Poyntz wrote a letter from Antwerp on August 25, 1535, addressed to his "well beloved brother John Poyntz, gentleman, dwelling in North Ockendon, Essex." Although directed to John, it was evident that Thomas intended for

---

24   Demaus, *William Tyndale*, 422–23.

25   Daniell, *William Tyndale*, 364.

26   Foxe, *Book of Martyrs*, 378.

27   Buxton, *At the House of Thomas Poyntz*, 34.

28   Foxe, *Acts and Monuments*, 5:123.

him to appeal on his behalf to influential contacts within his network, including Thomas Cromwell, King Henry VIII's secretary, who wielded considerable influence over administrative matters and the new Protestant English Church. The hurried style of the letter indicated Poyntz's urgency; he wanted John to grasp that Tyndale's execution seemed imminent and that his death would be "a great hinderance to the Gospel."

Thomas indicated that the king should be interested in identifying those in England who had encouraged Henry Phillips to pursue Tyndale. These individuals would likely oppose the Act of Supremacy that declared Henry as head of the English Church, implying that supporters of Tyndale's demise were disloyal to the king.[29] Ultimately, Poyntz's letter reached John, who relayed it to Thomas Cromwell, who then communicated the urgency to the king. Even before Cromwell received Poyntz's letter,[30] Cromwell dispatched his own messages to the Merchant-Adventurers, which Poyntz personally delivered to the high-level representatives at the council in Brussels.[31]

After waiting another three or four days, Poyntz learned that William Tyndale was supposed to be delivered to him. This news was a cause for rejoicing, but it was short-lived. Henry Phillips, having overheard the conversation, panicked; if Tyndale were freed, he would lose all hope of receiving his reward bounty.[32] The depth of Phillips's depravity was alarming. He had previously stolen from his own father and betrayed Tyndale; now he aimed to malign Tyndale's accomplice, Thomas Poyntz. To secure his bounty, Phillips accused Poyntz of being Tyndale's patron and sharing the same biblical convictions.[33]

29   Kingdon, *Incidents in the Lives*, unnumbered pages between pages 16–17.

30   Brian Buxton, "Thomas Poyntz: Defender of Tyndale," *Tyndale Society Journal* 27 (July 2004): online, accessed August 21, 2025, https://www.tyndale.org/journals/tsj27/buxton.html#id17.

31   Foxe, *Acts and Monuments*, 5:124.

32   Ibid.

33   Ibid.

Thomas Poyntz Arrested

On November 1, 1535, Thomas Poyntz was also arrested by Pierre Dufief and the emperor's attorney, following accusations made by Henry Phillips. Under oath, Poyntz was subjected to intense questioning about his faith and his knowledge of William Tyndale's teachings and supporters. The procurator general presented him with over twenty articles against Tyndale, each also applicable to Poyntz. These articles will be presented shortly; for now, it is enough to recognize that Poyntz was in grave danger—failure to comply could cost him everything. Prayer for wisdom was critical; now, more than ever, he needed the Lord's mercy to survive.

As the harsh winter of 1535 settled over Brussels, Thomas was granted the right to an attorney and was ordered to respond to the accusations within eight days. He could only send letters via the official Brussels mailing system and was restricted to writing in Dutch so that officials could scrutinize his correspondence. Speaking was also limited to Dutch.[34] On the eighth day, Poyntz provided vague answers that did not satisfy his inquisitors. As Foxe notes, "Thus he trifled them off, from Allhallow-tide until Christmas-even," procrastinating from "one eighth day to another eighth day."[35] His noncompliance frustrated both the accusers, and Poyntz felt deprived of the professional legal assistance promised to him. Jail officials demanded that Poyntz cover his confinement costs, but his attempts to raise funds were unsuccessful.

Given one more day to comply, he realized that failure to provide satisfactory answers would lead to more severe consequences. After more than three months in custody, Poyntz began to fear for his life. He believed that remaining under their control would lead to maximum security imprisonment with little hope of survival. Foxe's records

---

34   Foxe, *Acts and Monuments*, 125.

35   Ibid., 125–26.

detailing the specifics about Poyntz's escape are sparse, he simply writes, "In a night, by some means he conveyed himself off, and so, by God's help, at the opening of the town gate in the morning, he got away."[36] Thomas not only escaped from prison but also from Brussels itself. He eventually returned to England with nothing but his life and the clothes he wore during his escape. However, his escape marked the beginning of a new struggle that would last for another twenty years. Even for a businessman, living a godly life in Christ Jesus comes with consequences (2 Tim 3:12).

Thomas Poyntz Exiled

In February 1536, fleeing Brussels, Thomas left everything behind—a living illustration of Mark 10:28–31:

> And Petre began to saye unto him: Loo, we have forsaken all, and have folowed the. Jesus answered and sayde: Verely I saye unto you, there ys no man that hath forsaken house, or brethren, or sisters, or father, or moder, or wyfe, other chyldren, or londes, for my sake and the gospelles, whych shall nott receave an houndred foolde nowe in thys lyfe, houses, and brethrē, and sisters, and mothers and childrē, and londs whith persecucions, and in the worlde to come eternall lyfe. Many that are fyrste, shalbe last. And the last fyrst.

The North Sea separated him from his bride, Anna, and his four young children. His ability to earn a living was "annihilated; he could not resume it, for he was banished from the emperor's dominions."[37]

---

36   Foxe, *Acts and Monuments*, 5:127.

37   Kingdon, *Incidents in the Lives*, 20.

His home was no longer his haven or rest, as he faced persecution for his faith and for being a major supporter of William Tyndale.

Poyntz's attempts to bring his family to England were unsuccessful. His wife, Anna van Calva, a native of Flanders, rejected his efforts to reunite. Despite this, Thomas did not abandon his quest to be with his loved ones. He wrote to King Henry VIII, explaining that he had been banished from Antwerp five years earlier and that his wife refused to join him in England with their goods and children. He detailed his numerous appeals to her, but to no avail.[38]

When all else failed, Thomas invoked the Act of Naturalization, which granted rights to children born to the king's subjects overseas as if they were born within the realm. His petition was granted "[according to] the Statutes of the Realm ... there is recorded 'An Act for making free and to putt in the nature off mere Englishmen certayne children begotten and born byyonde the sea.'"[39]

Thomas won this legal battle, but it would take time for all his children to travel to England, and some may never have joined him. Frustrated, he returned to Antwerp at a great risk of imprisonment and death in order to earn a living and repair his broken marriage. However, Anna would never reunite with him.

Thomas's brother John died on June 13, 1547, leaving his estate to his wife, who was also named Anna, with the stipulation that Thomas would inherit his properties in North Ockendon upon her passing.[40] In 1554, Anna, John Poyntz' widow, died, leaving Thomas with the family estate until his own death in 1562. Thomas was buried near the grave of his sister-in-law, Anna Poyntz, on May 5, 1562, at St. Dunstan's in the West, the same church where Humphrey Monmouth heard William Tyndale preach from God's Word for the very first time in 1523.

---

38   Kingdon, *Incidents in the Lives*, 22.

39   Ibid., 21.

40   Maclean, *Memoir of the Family of Poyntz*, 33–34.

A Latin memorial to Thomas Poyntz at North Ockendon Church in Essex honors him for his sacrificial service to his beloved friend, for whom he risked his own neck (Rom 16:3):

Thomas Poyntz … for faithful service to his prince and ardent profession of the evangelical truth suffered chains and imprisonment in regions across the seas plainly already destined to be killed except he himself trusting in divine providence looked for a miraculous escape from prison.[41]

Though Poyntz feared that the loss of Tyndale would be "a great hinderance to the Gospel," the opposite occurred; the gospel advanced, as it always does under persecution.

Poyntz's support of William Tyndale became one of the most significant advancements of the gospel in the sixteenth century and a gift to countless future generations not only for English readers, but also for those in many other languages.

"Lord, Open the King of England's Eyes!"

On April 13, 1536, Stephen Vaughn, an English merchant commissioned by Thomas Cromwell to persuade William Tyndale to return to England, wrote to Cromwell. He believed his efforts would be fruitful if Cromwell could convince the legal authorities in Brussels to spare Tyndale from the flames. Unfortunately, his plea was in vain. Sparing Tyndale's life was overshadowed by King Henry's preoccupation with the death of Catherine of Aragon in January 1536 and with Anne Boleyn's miscarriage of the king's heir. Amidst accusations of Queen Anne's infidelity, Henry relied on Cromwell to investigate.

---

41   Brian Buxton, "Thomas Poyntz: Brought Unto Misery for so Godly a Cause," *Tyndale Society Journal* 24 (Apr 2003): online, accessed August 21, 2025, https://www.tyndale.org/journals/tsj24/buxton.html.

Thus, Cromwell, along with divesting monastery lands, became busy with facilitating the dissolution of Henry's second marriage in order to pursue another woman, Jane Seymour. Given these pressing matters, it is easy to understand why Thomas Poyntz' previous cries for help had gone unheard.

All human attempts to save William Tyndale were futile. Not even the influential Poyntz family could prevent his martyrdom. After spending a year and a half in the Castle Vilvoorde prison, Tyndale faced the charges read against him. Although the specific charges have not survived, Demaus outlines the seven common accusations levied against Lutheran "heretics": 1) the belief that faith alone justifies; 2) believing that there is forgiveness of sins and that mercy is offered in the gospel as being sufficient for salvation; 3) the assertion that human traditions do not bind the conscience; 4) the denial of the freedom of the will; 5) the rejection of purgatory; 6) the belief that neither Jesus' mother, Mary, nor the saints pray for people; and 7) the insistence that people should not pray to Mary or Roman Catholic saints.[42]

After being found guilty, the emperor condemned William Tyndale to death. He was escorted to the execution site, where the executioner bound him to a stake and placed a chain around his neck. William Tyndale was prepared to die; his last words suggest his thoughts were on the refined edits he made to 1 Timothy 2:1–2:

> I exhorte therfore that above all thynges prayeers, supplicacions, peticions, and gevynge of thankes, behad for all men: for kinges, and for all thatt are in preeminēce, thatt we maye live a quyet and a peasable life, in all godlines and honestie.

---

42 Demaus, William Tyndale, 458–59.

Ever since the time of his employment with Sir John and Lady Anne Walsh in 1522, Tyndale longed for God's Word to be available to his people. He must have prayed numerous times for the Lord to move King Henry VIII to grant the printing of English Bibles in England. Such a righteous prayer ultimately became Tyndale's last words. Just before the chain tightened, William Tyndale cried out to his Savior, praying "Lord! Open the king of England's eyes."[43] Then, Pierre Dufief, Procurator-General, ordered Tyndale to be strangled. Once it was clear that he was dead, they ignited the straw and gunpowder, consuming the earthly remains of the heaven-present William Tyndale. Absent from his body, his faith was now sight, and he was at home with his Lord (2 Cor 5:7–8).

---

43   Foxe, *Acts and Monuments*, 5:126–27. See the sketch of William Tyndale at the stake.

Conclusion

This journey through church history recounted how William Tyndale and his fellow workers in the truth risked everything to produce and distribute the English Bible. The unique role the Lord assigns to His people working in the marketplace to advance the Great Commission is a profound blessing. While theirs is an adventure filled with success, exhilaration, and courage, along with blessing and honor, it also comes with pain, sorrow, and grief. However, those who walk worthily of their calling accept the responsibility, knowing that they too may suffer for the sake of the gospel (John 16:1–4).

From the Holy Spirit–inspired letters and books that the apostles and prophets wrote in the New Testament, we know that God gave gifts to the church in the form of pastors, teachers, and evangelists to exposit their inerrant texts so that the saints in their churches would be equipped to do the work of the ministry (Eph 4:11–16).

Men like Tyndale prepared subsequent generations to translate the same ancient biblical Greek and Hebrew texts so that people speaking the languages of the world would be exposed to the Word of God. It is a pastor's responsibility to "be diligent to present [himself] approved to God as a workman who does not need to be ashamed, accurately handling the word of truth" (2 Tim 2:15). This requires him to be a trained exegete who can handle God's Word authoritatively, so that he can preach the original author's intent with precision, power, and passion, resulting in the saints under his shepherding care doing the work of the ministry. Pastors, just like Timothy, must train subsequent generations of shepherds to do the same—who, in turn, would train still more generations of men to equip the saints in their churches (2 Tim 2:2).

Currently, there are thousands of languages devoid of Scripture translated from Greek and Hebrew. Our generation must train qualified

young men who are already fluent in their own languages to exegete
Greek and Hebrew so that they can translate the Bible into their own
tongues. It is insufficient to translate the Bible from languages other
than the original biblical texts. Doing so opens the door to much confusion and unintended mistakes, many of which result in heresy and false
converts. The challenge is for biblically qualified men to accept the call
to be trained and mentored in biblical hermeneutics, languages, exegesis, doctrine, shepherding, pastoral ministry, and expository preaching.

None of those requirements are possible without fellow workers
in the truth equally accepting the call of God to support their training. As in Tyndale's day, it may require significant sacrifice, even risking
one's own life to ensure that qualified men are constantly prayed for and
that they can afford their training. Whether you are a business administrator, logistics expert, widow, government official, brickmaker, chief
executive, salesperson, law enforcement officer, stay-at-home mom, or
of any other profession, God's call for you is to reach the nations of the
world with the gospel of Christ until the end of the age.

Have you considered that your link in this mission might be to pray
for and support your brothers and sisters on the front lines in places
you may never visit? Has God enabled you to support the translation of the Bible from its original languages? What about connecting
with those who are translating biblically sound theological works into
foreign dialects?

As you celebrate the 500th anniversary of William Tyndale's New
Testaments arriving in England and engage with this historical account
of Tyndale and his associates, I pray that you would consider how God
may be moving you to be another link in His supply chain. Please ask
the Lord to guide your service to Him, using your skills and expertise
in the marketplace and public square. Not all Christians must go to a
foreign nation to serve Him, but all Christians must fulfill the Great
Commission by communicating the Word of God and using their gifts,
skills, and expertise to make disciples of all nations.

Thus, dear readers, this is my prayer for you: that you would coura-geously serve Christ so that future generations will glorify the Lord.

Be encouraged by the Apostle Paul's humble approach to serving his Savior so that Tyndale's contemporaries, and now our generation, would know the Lord:

And nowe beholde I goo bounde in the sprete unto Jerusalem,
and knowe nott what shall come off me there, butt that the holy gost
witnesseth in every cite sayinge: that bondes and trouble abyde me: but
none of tho thinges move me. Nether is my lyfe dere unto my silfe, that
I myght fulfill my course with ioye, ād the ministracion which I have
receaved of the lorde Iesu to testify the gospell of the grace of god.
Acts 20:22–24

Bibliography

Alford, Stephen. *London's Triumph: Merchants, Adventurers, and Money in Shakespeare's City*. New York: Bloomsbury USA, 2017.

Amyot, Thomas. "Transcript of an Original Manuscript, Containing a Memorial from George Constantyne to Thomas Lord Cromwell." In *Archaeologia: or, Miscellaneous Tracts Relating to Antiquity*. London: Society of Antiquaries of London, 1831. Accessed at Internet Archive. https://archive.org/details/s2id13276820/page/50/mode/2up.

Arndt, William, Frederick W. Danker, Walter Bauer, and F. Wilbur Gingrich. *A Greek-English Lexicon of the New Testament and Other Early Christian Literature*. 3rd ed. Chicago: University of Chicago Press, 2000.

Ballitch, Andrew S. "Worms, Diet Of." In *The Essential Lexham Dictionary of Church History*, edited by Michael A. G. Haykin. Bellingham, WA: Lexham Press, 2022.

Bertheau, Carl. "Schuldorp, Marquard." In *Allgemeine Deutsche Biographie*. Vol. 32, 657–58. Leipzig: Verlag von Dunder & Humblot, 1891. Accessed at Internet Archive.

Brigden, Susan. *London and the Reformation*. London: Faber & Faber, 1989.

Butterworth, Charles C., and Allan G. Chester. *George Joye: 1495?–1553: A Chapter in the History of the English Bible and the English Reformation*. Philadelphia: University of Pennsylvania Press, 1962.

Buxton, Brian. *At the House of Thomas Poyntz: The Betrayal of William Tyndale with the Consequences for an English Merchant and His Family*. Lavenham, UK: Brian Buxton, 2013.

_____. "Thomas Poyntz: Defender of Tyndale." *Tyndale Society Journal* 27 (July 2004): online [21–28]. Accessed August 21, 2025. https://www.tyndale.org/journals/tsj27/buxton.html#id17.

_____."Thomas Poyntz: Brought Unto Misery for so Godly a Cause." *Tyndale Society Journal* 24 (Apr 2003): online [8–21]. Accessed August 21, 2025. https://www.tyndale.org/journals/tsj24/buxton.html.

Casson, Lionel. *Travel in the Ancient World.* 1974. Reprint, Baltimore: The Johns Hopkins University Press, 1994.

Collinson, Patrick, and John Craig, eds. *The Reformation in English Towns, 1500–1640.* New York: St. Martin's Press, 1998.

Daniell, David. *William Tyndale: A Biography.* New Haven, CT: Yale University Press, 2001.

Deanesly, Margaret. *The Lollard Bible and Other Medieval Biblical Versions.* Cambridge: Cambridge University Press, 1920. Accessed at Hathi Trust. https://babel.hathitrust.org/cgi/pt?id=yale.39002012 664828&seq=1.

Demaus, Robert. *William Tyndale: A Biography.* London: The Religious Tract Society, [1871].

Dollinger, Philippe. *The German Hansa.* Translated by D. S. Ayalon and S. H. Winston. Stanford, CA: Stanford University Press, 1970. Accessed at Internet Archive. https://archive.org/details/germanhansa0000doll.

Elwell, Walter A., and Philip Wesley Comfort. *Tyndale Bible Dictionary.* Tyndale Reference Library. Wheaton, IL: Tyndale House Publishers, 2001.

Erasmus, Desiderius. *Enchiridion Militis Christiani.* Translated anonymously. London: Methuen & Co., 1905. Accessed at The Online Library of Liberty. https://oll.libertyfund.org/titles/erasmus-the-manual-of-a-christian-knight.

Farris, Michael. *From Tyndale to Madison: How the Death of an English Martyr Led to the American Bill of Rights.* Nashville: B&H Publishing Group, 2007.

Foxe, John. *Foxe's Book of Martyrs: A History of the Lives, Sufferings and Triumphant Deaths of the Early Christian and Protestant Martyrs.* Edited by William Byron Forbush. New York: Holt, Rinehart, and Winston, 1954.

_____. *The Acts and Monuments of John Foxe.* 8 vols. London: R. B. Seeley and W. Burnside, 1837–1839. Accessed at Internet Archive.

Gamble, Harry Y. *Books and Readers in the Early Church: A History of Early Christian Texts.* New Haven, CT: Yale University Press, 1995.

Gasquet, Francis Aidan. *The Eve of the Reformation: Studies in the Religious Life and Thought of the English People in the Period Preceding the Rejection of the Roman Jurisdiction by Henry VIII.* New York: G. P. Putnam's Sons, 1900.

Gleason, John B. *John Colet.* Berkeley: University of California Press, 1989.

Gwyn, Peter. *The King's Cardinal: The Rise and Fall of Thomas Wolsey.* London: Barrie & Jenkins, 1990.

Hope, Andrew. "Thomas More and Humphrey Monmouth: Conscience and Coercion in Reformation England." In *Theorizing Legal Personhood in Late Medieval England,* edited by Andreea D. Boboc, 235–56. Medieval Law and Its Practice 18. Leiden: Brill, 2015.

Horn, Joyce M., ed. *Fasti Ecclesiae Anglicanae 1300–1541. Volume 5, St Paul's, London.* London: Institute of Historical Research, 1963. British History Online. Accessed August 21, 2025. https://www.british-history.ac.uk/fasti-ecclesiae/1300-1541/vol5/pp1-4#fnn4.

Hoyle, R. W. *Military Survey of Gloucestershire, 1522.* Stroud, Great Britain: Bristol and Gloucestershire Archaeological Society, 1993.

Inwood, Stephen. *A History of London*. London: Macmillan, 1998.

Johnson, Jesse. *City of Man, Kingdom of God: Why Christians Respect, Obey, and Resist Government*. Pennsauken, NJ: BookBaby, 2022.

Jones, Evan T. *Inside the Illicit Economy: Reconstructing the Smugglers' Trade of Sixteenth Century Bristol*. New York: Routledge, 2016.

Kingdon, John Abernathy. *Incidents in the Lives of Thomas Poyntz and Richard Grafton*. London: Privately Printed by Rixon & Arnold, 1895.

Lee, John S. "Working in the Middle Ages: The Medieval Clothier." Medievalists.net. September 2018. Accessed May 15, 2025. https://www.medievalists.net/2018/09/working-in-the-middle-ages-the-medieval-clothier/.

Legacy Standard Bible. Irvine, CA: Three Sixteen Publishing, 2022.

Loane, Marcus. *Masters of the English Reformation*. 1954. Reprint, Edinburgh: Banner of Truth Trust, 2005.

Luther, Martin. *The Freedom of a Christian*. Translated by Robert Kolb. Wheaton, IL: Crossway, 2023.

MacArthur, John, and Richard Mayhue, eds. *Biblical Doctrine: A Systematic Summary of Bible Truth*. Wheaton, IL: Crossway, 2017.

MacArthur, John. *Romans 9–16*. The MacArthur New Testament Commentary. Chicago: Moody Publishers, 1994.

Maclean, John. *Historical and Genealogical Account of the Family of Poyntz*. Exeter: William Pollard, 1886. Accessed at Internet Archive. https://archive.org/details/historicalgeneal01macl/page/34/mode/2up.

Maclean, John, ed. "Transactions of the Bristol and Gloucestershire Archaeological Society in 1888–9, Proceedings at the Spring Meeting at Chipping Sodbury, On Tuesday, May 29th, 1888." *Transactions of the Bristol and Gloucestershire Archaeological Society* 13 (1888–89): 1–5. Accessed at Internet Archive.

Magnus Albertus. *De Secretis Mulierum: Or, the Mysteries of Human Generation Fully Revealed.* Translated by John Quincy. London: Printed for E. Curll, 1725. Accessed at Internet Archive.

Moo, Douglas J. *The Epistle to the Romans.* The New International Commentary on the New Testament. Grand Rapids: Wm. B. Eerdmans, 1996.

Morris, Leon. *The Epistle to the Romans.* The Pillar New Testament Commentary. Grand Rapids: Wm. B. Eerdmans, 1988.

Moynahan, Brian. *God's Bestseller.* New York: St. Martin's Press, 2003.

Mozley, J. F. *William Tyndale.* New York: The Macmillan Company, 1937.

Newe Testament, The. [Translated by William Tyndale. Worms, Germany: Peter Schoeffer], 1526.

Strype, John. *Ecclesiastical Memorials, Relating Chiefly to Religion and the Reformation of It, and the Emergencies of the Church of England, under King Henry VIII, King Edward VI, and Queen Mary I, with Large Appendixes, Containing Original Papers, Records, &c.* Vol. 1, Pts. 1–2. Oxford: Clarendon Press, 1822. Accessed at Internet Archive.

_____. *Memorials of the Most Reverend Father in God Thomas Cranmer, Sometime Lord Archbishop of Canterbury.* Vol. 1. Oxford: Oxford University Press, 1840. Accessed at Google Books.

Tyndale, William. *The 1536 Tyndale Bible New Testament.* 1536.

_____. *The Pentateuch.* Translated by William Tyndale. Marburg, Hesse: Hans Lufft, 1530. Accessed at Internet Archive. https://archive.org/details/1530-tyndale-pentateuch/page/n7/mode/2up.

_____. *Tyndale's New Testament: A Modern-Spelling Edition of the 1534 Translation.* Edited by David Daniell. New Haven, CT: Yale University Press, 1989.

_____. *The Works of William Tyndale*. Vol. 1, *Doctrinal Treatises and Introductions to Different Portions of the Holy Scriptures*. 1848. Reprint, Edinburgh: Banner of Truth Trust, 2010.

_____. *The Works of William Tyndale*. Vol. 2, *Expositions and Notes on Sundry Portions of the Holy Scriptures, together with The Practice of Prelates*. 1849. Reprint, Edinburgh: Banner of Truth Trust, 2010.

Tzeses, Jennifer. "King Henry VIII and Anne Boleyn Lived in This $10.5 Million Castle." Architectural Digest, August 2, 2016. https://www.architecturaldigest.com/story/king-henry-viii-anne-boleyn-castle.

Weathers, Eric. "Shrewdly Investing in the Great Commission: The Parable in Luke 16:1–13." In *Biblical Missions: Principles, Priorities, Practices*, edited by Mark Tatlock and Chris Burnett, 319–25. Nashville: Thomas Nelson, 2025.

_____. "Holding the Rope: 3 John for Missions Donors." In *Biblical Missions: Principles, Priorities, Practices*, edited by Mark Tatlock and Chris Burnett, 345–52. Nashville: Thomas Nelson, 2025.

Webster, William. *The Church of Rome at the Bar of History*. Edinburgh: Banner of Truth Trust, 1995.

Wheeler, Heather Y. *King Henry VIII Coronation 24th June 1509*. Tudor Nation. Last Updated July 12, 2024. https://www.tudornation.com/king-henry-viii-coronation.

XE.com. *Currency Converter: GBP to USD*. Accessed May 19, 2025. https://www.xe.com/currencyconverter/convert/?Amount=15052.88&From=GBP&To=USD.

Zeidan, Adam. "Languages by Total Number of Speakers." In *Encyclopædia Britannica*. Accessed May 15, 2025. https://www.britannica.com/topic/languages-by-total-number-of-speakers-2228881.

Zodhiates, Spiros, comp. and ed. *The Complete Word Study Dictionary: New Testament*. Iowa Falls, IA: World Bible Publishers, 1992.

The Master's Academy International is committed to fulfilling the Great Commission by training indigenous church leaders to be approved pastor-teachers, able to equip their churches to make biblically sound disciples.

THE
MASTER'S ACADEMY
INTERNATIONAL

tmai.org

www.ingramcontent.com/pod-product-compliance
Lightning Source LLC
LaVergne TN
LVHW020054090426
835513LV00030B/2202